Buried Deep in My Heart

Also by the same author:

Glimpses – (2007) The London Press

Buried Deep in My Heart

By

DECLAN HENRY

THE LONDON PRESS

Buried Deep in My Heart

First published by The London Press, UK 2010

Copyright © Declan Henry 2010

The right of Declan Henry to be identified as the author of
this work has been asserted by him in accordance with the Copyright,
Designs and Patents Act 1988.

All rights reserved. No part of this publication may be reproduced,
stored in or introduced into a retrieval system, or transmitted, in any
form, or by means (electronic, mechanical, photocopying, recording or
otherwise) without the prior written permission of the publisher.
Any person who does any unauthorised act in relation to this
publication may be liable to criminal prosecution or
civil claims for damages.

ISBN: 978-1-907313-75-2

A C.I.P. reference is available from the British Library.

Printed and bound in Great Britain by
CPI Antony Rowe, Chippenham and Eastbourne

Disclaimer

The author has changed the names of teachers and
several other people featured in the book in order to
protect their identity.

This book is dedicated to my late brother Padraic

Contents

Introduction   xi

1 Earlier Times   1

2 Rural Happenings   19

3 St Joseph's   36

4 Defining Moments of Christmas   53

5 Why Priest?   60

6 Saved by the Bell   72

7 Music was the Breath of Life   85

8 Events to Amuse, Entertain and Occupy   93

9 And Then there were Three   113

10 The Pope's visit to Knock   122

11 Time to Move On   127

   Acknowledgements   138

   About the Author   139

Introduction by Joe Byrne

Ceol agus Ealaion, (The Music and Arts Show) Midwest Radio Mayo, Ireland

Reeling in the Years is the title of an RTE – Irish Television – series of programmes which dip into archival TV film footage covering the past four or five decades. Each programme offers year-by-year glimpses of the way we used to be, with snapshots of working lives, sports, politics, fashions, and singular events, all shown with accompanying pop music anthems from that era. The series clearly demonstrates the unprecedented amount of changes that were compressed into the Ireland of 1960s to the 1990s. The old reels graphically capture those images of a changing Ireland in a special way, and yet it is ironical to reflect that the station itself was one of the leading agents that helped to bring about several of those changes.

Declan Henry's birth in the 1960s almost coincides with the birth of RTE – Ireland's first national television channel – and in a sense many of the lines in this book of memoirs could easily be deployed as a script for the *Reeling in the Years* series, as he describes growing up on the Mayo-Sligo border up until 1981, when he left for Galway and third-level college. In this book, sketches from rural life in Derrykinlough mirror the changing scene that came with Ireland's membership of the European Economic Community, and with the moderate increases in prosperity that ensued. Monetary savings began to change into disposable income, borrowing money became easier, and as the Americans were launching their spacecrafts towards the moon, Ireland was being launched on a pathway to becoming a modern consumer society, while a drastic decline in the rural population continued.

The early chapters of this memoir dwell on the more traditional ways of life. Farm practices, such as the saving of hay and turf, are detailed, as well as home produce and home cooking – and so also is the move away from manual work as farm machinery, motor vehicles and domestic appliances were purchased. A tractor, a van, a modest extension and some alterations to the family home and garden were savoured as novel pleasures in the Henry household.

The social and community dynamic undergoes phenomenal changes, and these are also reflected upon in the memoir. For generations this area had an exceptionally rich tradition in music, song, dance and lore with marching bands, house and small-hall dances, stage productions, sports and gatherings – an involved neighbourhood that entertained itself. Because of emigration and the shrinking numbers of young people, many of those local forms of interaction and entertainment were eventually substituted or sidelined. For example, three of the many celebrated musicians from that part of east Mayo were making music and names for themselves elsewhere by night and then working on building sites during the day to make ends meet. Brendan Tonra, the noted fiddle player and composer, was in Boston. Piper and actor Kevin Henry was in Chicago, and Roger Sherlock, the flute player, was packing them in at The Hibernian Club in Fulham and The Galtymore in Cricklewood. At home in the author's household, however, like so many other households of the time, it was the radio, popular records, television, the junior columns of the *St Martin Magazine*, and the papers his father sent from England that mostly attracted young Declan's attention. *Nothing Ever Happens in Carmincross*, the title of Benedict Kiely's novel comes to mind, and in a way that title sums up what was going on – or not going on – in the remote townlands of Derrykinlough and Brackloon and in so many other townlands all over Ireland in those years. The real action was, for the most part, somewhere else.

There was some entertainment to be had in the general hinterland, of course. There is mention of efforts to set up a community and youth centre, weekend visits to Kennedy's 'singing pub-lounge' in nearby Doocastle, uncomfortable nights at showband dances in Charlestown and, a little later, the flicker of the first disco lights in the area.

The Catholic Church and the clergy were of course a significant influence, and the Henrys, again like so many others, were regular churchgoers. Declan did stints as an altar boy and though deemed by many to be an ideal candidate for the priesthood, he didn't really consider the idea – another sign perhaps of the rising winds of change during the 1970s.

There are glimpses from the local primary school in Rooskey, and from the secondary school in Tubbercurry, but it is interesting that the first seeds for real writing were sown not in school but at home. Letter writing was a central part of those decades before telephones in the home became the norm, so Declan wrote weekly letters detailing family and local news to his father, who worked seasonally for a number of months each year in England.

References to personal family life, such as the tragic accident that took the life of his brother Padraic while working in Scotland, are woven occasionally into the narrative.

Written in a clear straightforward manner, this memoir gives interesting snapshots of rural Ireland during the decades before the so-called 'Celtic Tiger' was unleashed on the land. We travel from a time when Nora's front door was always open during the day, when there was the novelty of the odd trips to town, the arrival of the first artificial Christmas tree in the home during his early teens and, towards the end, a time when the author deliberately tried to fail an interview for a third-level course.

In conclusion, this book certainly has an unmistakable ring of authenticity and honesty about it.

I

Earlier Times

There is a story behind every photograph, but a childhood photograph is always the most unique because it signifies the beginning of a journey. For some children, this journey will consist of happiness, wonderment and discovery, while others will encounter misery, loneliness and rejection. My own journey in life, which was to prove an interesting voyage, began on a farm in a quiet country village in the west of Ireland named Derrykinlough. Situated on the Mayo-Sligo border in the province of Connaught, I was to grow up and spend the first eighteen years of my life there.

There are two photographs, both taken in the sixties, which show my brothers and I in joyous mood. One was taken when I was two years old, and the other when I was aged five. My eldest brother, John, was ten years older than me, Kevin, eight years older, and Padraic, six years older. In the photographs we are standing in a line in ascending order according to our ages and height, and I feel these photographs highlight the start of us growing up together as a family. Our different personalities – some outgoing, some reserved – combined with each of us having different coloured hair, made us wonder if we actually came from the same parents. On top of this, I received merciless teasing from my brothers. They claimed I was adopted, which would account for my perceived difference to them, and combined this with comments like 'definitely the wrong baby' in reference to a claim that my mother had mistakenly taken somebody else's baby home from the nursing home after giving birth. Either way, I was left with a feeling that one day someone would knock on the door demanding my return! It was all intended as harmless fun, however, and the joking didn't leave me with any lasting scars.

It was a cold Thursday morning in December when I was born in the St John of God Nursing Home in Ballymote, a rural farming town in County Sligo ten miles from our home. The town became synonymous with my family's history, as my three brothers also came into the world there. Close to the nursing home is the Church of the Immaculate Conception, where I was baptised, and right next door stood the ruins of a thirteenth-century castle which, according to the history books, was built by Richard de Burgo (the second Earl of Ulster) – more commonly known at the time as the 'Red Earl' because of his mane of red hair. The earl was apparently a formidable character who, over the course of his life, forcibly gained entitlement to almost half the lands of Ireland and was thus considered the most prominent property owner in the country. His prominence began at the time of the English invasion in Ireland, but people seldom refer to him any more and most people, apart from historians, have never even heard of him. But exist he did, and his castle in Ballymote was most impressive. The embittered times in which the earl lived are well and truly over, but this impressive piece of medieval architecture still remains, although it is now nothing more than a well-preserved ruin.

My mother was discharged from the nursing home six days after I was born, and as it wasn't long before Christmas, a christening was planned for the day she was allowed home. Johnny Durkin, a neighbour and friend of my father, was chosen as my godfather, with my first cousin Mary Clossick as my godmother. My mother decided on the name 'Declan' from the suggestions given to her by the nuns at the nursing home. 'Damien' was suggested as an alternative, but my mother didn't like it, and so it was immediately dismissed. My father chose 'Gerard' as my middle name – I have no idea why. It was a simple service with just my parents, godparents, brothers and some of the nuns from the nursing home present to see me receive my 'licence of identity' and to thereafter be known as 'Declan Gerard Henry'.

Ballymote was a fairly big town by the standards of the day with several shops, including two supermarkets, three drapers' shops, a newsagent, a hardware shop, and numerous public houses. But what made the town unique from other towns was its train station, and it was well frequented for this purpose alone.

A trip to Ballymote usually entailed a visit to my father's cousin, Maria O'Dowd, and her husband, Jackie. This was always a source of enjoyment, and Maria always made us feel so welcome whenever we visited. She had spent most of her early life in the United States, and not only did she have an American accent, she had also inherited some of their customs. There was always something new to notice or learn at Maria's. She always used the best linen and china when entertaining us, and if she didn't have enough food, being an ever-gracious hostess, she would quickly dispatch Jackie to the shops to get more. Another fascination for me when visiting the O'Dowds was using their bathroom. The cistern of the toilet was placed high on the wall over the toilet bowl and had an amazingly long chain attached to it, making it very different and much more interesting to a young boy than the one we had at home.

Ballymote even had its own hotel, The Dinette Hotel, which was considered quite luxurious with its green décor and matching carpets. We often went there for refreshments. It wasn't really that posh, but I always felt important whenever we went there, and as it was the only hotel I visited in my younger years, I had no other image with which to compare it. On one occasion we went into the main dining room for lunch. Roast lamb was the main dish on the menu so we decided to order that. I still remember sitting in the dining room eagerly looking up every time the kitchen door opened to see if the food was coming. But the anticipation was worth it because after what seemed to be endless hours of waiting and combating hunger, our lunch finally arrived and it was simply delicious.

The Gaelic name for Derrykinlough is 'Doire Cinn Locha', meaning 'Oak Wood at the Head of a Lake'. It comprised of 560 acres, of which nearly 300 were marshland. Being a rugged part of the west of Ireland, it was incredibly beautiful in summer, but like most country landscapes, it could look sombre and bleak in winter. The village was fortunate enough to have had its own lake, which was rather scenic all year round, especially as it was home to several swans whose serene presence graced it almost every day. This sight was enhanced by the occasional fisherman fishing for pike, and the odd rowing boat sailing from one shore to the other – a distance of just over half a mile.

But one of the most extraordinary things about Derrykinlough was the spelling of its name. It was very much like a Shakespearean dilemma of 'to use a "y" or not to use a "y"' – or 'to use one "r" or two "r"s'. There were three different ways to spell it: 'Derrykinlough', 'Derrikinlough' or 'Derikinlough'. During my primary school years I was taught to spell it 'Derrikinlough', but then when I transferred to secondary school it switched over to 'Derrykinlough', and I have spelt it this way ever since!

Nevertheless, the intrigue of the spelling didn't end there. An old school master told my brothers that it didn't matter if the village was spelt with one 'r' or two, provided that it was never spelt with a 'y' in the middle because this would automatically confuse people into believing that the village had some connection to County Derry in Northern Ireland. Was this possible, I wonder? Well, I guess there are people in society who are not so knowledgeable with their geography. Anyhow, my brothers took the master's advice and avoided the prospects of any future faux pas with the spelling. One would have thought that the definitive answer to the spelling could have been found in the official parish records, which spelt it 'Derrykinlough', but confusion and conflict ensued with some people categorically stating that the parish records contained the wrong spelling. Perhaps my grandfather, Thomas Henry, was one of those people who contested these records because I have seen a letter he once wrote, and his preferred spelling was 'Derikinlough'. How he settled on this spelling is a mystery, and like the Shakespearean question, it remains unanswered!

Life in Derrykinlough was very rural, but so too was life in every other village in the community. Everyone lived their lives in similar circumstances to those of my family. Some households were a little richer, others a little poorer, but in the main we were all very similar to one another and there was no class division. Our nearest neighbours were almost a mile away on either side of our home, and this isolation provided a fair degree of tranquillity in itself. We had lovely neighbours though. I especially remember Mary Ellen who visited our house every week when she cycled to the post office to collect her pension. She always bought me sweets, and I was often to be found on the road outside our house waiting for her to arrive. Some people's kindness is never forgotten and I will always remember Mary Ellen. Our local church, St Joseph's, was a mile and a half away, and we had two public houses, a shop, and the post office in neighbouring villages. Derrykinlough once had its own primary school. My father and his sisters were educated there as well as my three brothers for a time before it closed in 1966 because of a dwindling number of pupils.

Once a week we had access to Des Corcoran's mobile shop, where we could buy everything from sugar to shoelaces. Des tried his best to ensure his travelling shop arrived at a fixed time and on the same day every week, but this didn't always go to plan since he had a busy and demanding business resulting in him sometimes not turning up until the next day. Nevertheless, it was a case of either waiting for him to come or hiring a car to go to town. We also had a very reliable bread man who came twice weekly on Mondays and Fridays. His name was Peter Brett, and his wife was a first cousin to my father. I am not praising him just because of his family connection; he genuinely was a lovely, friendly man, and there was always a wonderful fresh smell of baking oozing from his van, which was filled with a variety of breads and cakes.

My father had an uncle he was very fond of who he called 'Jimmy Seamus'. His real name was James Ryan, brother of my paternal grandmother. He had a reputation for having a great sense of humour and was constantly spoken about affectionately in our house. He was especially notable for his frequent wisecracks and pearls of wisdom. One of his favourite sayings at Christmas time was to raise his glass of whiskey and make a toast: 'Well, if we are no better off this time next year, let's hope that we're no worse!'

I liked visiting Jimmy Seamus's house with my parents and brothers because he and his wife always extended us such a wonderfully warm welcome. We didn't go very often, but when we did, we were always given lovely things to eat. As a child it was great being entertained outside the family home and being given a different variety of cake or treat which we perhaps hadn't tried at home.

However, getting to Jimmy Seamus's house was like trying to get into a Chinese box. It was in a very remote and isolated spot, and to get there you had to go down a 'boreen' road – basically a track – for half a mile, then follow a track through several fields. It was a matter of opening and shutting gates to various fields before eventually arriving at the house, which had lovely trees and a stream at its back.

Though tricky at times, this route to Jimmy Seamus's did provide ample opportunity to see the many variants of wild flowers that grew in abundance in the local countryside. It was not unusual to see a multitude of different species, which varied with the changing of the seasons. Spring brought clumps of gorse bushes with their distinctive yellow colour and coconut scent. The paler primroses, which grew in profusion everywhere, complemented these. In summertime a variety of wild poppies erupted in the clover in glimmering pink, lilac and purple. Wild unnamed plants resembling cauliflowers but smelling of vanilla were half-interred amongst the copious ferns alongside nettles, heather and dock leaves. There were the ever-visible thistles, dandelions, buttercups, and daisies growing wild at the foot of hedgerows and ditches, and growing amongst all of these were white berries. A myth surrounded these berries, with some people believing that cows wouldn't eat them because they were poisonous, but I never heard of any fatalities. In fact, I occasionally used to pick one of the berries and burst it to see what they were like on the inside, only to be disgusted each time by its foul smell. Late summer would bring blossoms to the elderberry trees and blackberry bushes that grew wild on any spare piece of land that contained briers or bramble.

I was six years old when Jimmy Seamus suddenly died of a heart attack. When he passed away I remember going to his home with my family to pay our respects and to view the body. He was the first dead person I had ever seen, and it was a frightening experience for a six-year-old. Jimmy looked so unfamiliar in the coffin, and I noticed that he looked very white and very cold. He was barely recognisable as the man I knew and loved, especially without his spectacles. I looked around the room and noticed that they had been placed on the mantelpiece over the fireplace. It took me quite a while to get over the fright of seeing a dead body for the first time. I am not exactly certain of how long I was afraid of being in the dark afterwards, even though I shared a bed with one of my brothers, but I am sure this experience was no different to any other child who sees a dead person for the first time. Death has always been very real and a big part of Irish life and from an early age seeing dead people and regularly attending funerals exposed me to mortality in a very open and revealing way.

My father held vague recollections of stories he had heard from his grandparents about the post-famine era in Ireland. These pertained to our ancestors who had lived through the pain and suffering of probably the worst disaster in Irish history – the Famine of 1846, which resulted in four million people, half the population, being starved to death. Many of our ancestors held understandable bitterness towards the English for refusing to help Ireland during this time.

There was a forest next to Derrykinlough Lake that held deep in its midst the ruins of an old stone cottage built before the famine. Getting to the derelict cottage was never easy, as you had to make your way through some fields which followed a strip of land by a stream. Closer to the forest there were briers everywhere, so you had to take care not to get caught up in them. You then had to be doubly careful of the overgrown grass, which hid the occasional swamp underneath the moss and heather at the edge of the forest. If you did get caught, you ended up waist-deep in mud. However, the effort of getting there was well worth it because you were immediately greeted by a great sense of calmness and peace once inside the forest.

The cottage, which consisted of no more than two or three rooms, had stone-crafted gables with the front and back still intact. The ruins of the front door and two fireplaces inside were similar. It had three windows at the front but none at the back, and there were several out-houses, also built from stone.

There seemed to be a strange air of mystery surrounding the cottage, partly perhaps because it was seldom visited – only a handful of people even knew of its existence. It had, as it were, become a forgotten monument to the past, hidden well away from view. As a young boy I was rather attached to the place and often questioned my father about the people who had once lived there. Unfortunately, he knew very little about the last inhabitants of the cottage, which was hardly surprising since it had lain derelict for over a hundred years. Parish records were destroyed during the famine, making it more difficult to learn about the people who had lived there and the enormous struggle they must have endured in surviving the horrific starvation that destroyed so many lives.

We all need a sense of belonging to somewhere – and indeed to some-one. I was the youngest of my parents' four sons and was very fortunate to have a great mother and father who provided me with very good role models. Both of them created a wonderful sense of security and stability for my brothers and me. I never experienced poverty, domestic violence or any neglect in my home. I never saw my parents drunk, and I even struggle to remember them ever having an argument.

Families still spent a lot of time together at home when I was a child, and irrespective of what meal we were having, my mother would always set the table properly. It was taken for granted that we all attended Mass together on Sundays, and it was inconceivable for my brothers or I to make an excuse not to attend. This was more or less the same with attending school, with extreme sickness being the only reason for not going. Routines of this kind led to obedience and respect for parents, school, church and elders in our community.

My mother, Kathleen, was an avid reader, who showed a great interest in life and in the people around her. She always had a youthful attitude that made her a humorous, kind and loving person. My mother was the youngest of five children, and her mother, Ann Callaghan, died suddenly when she was just six months old. Her father, Edward Callaghan, was a farmer who found it difficult having to raise a young family alone, which resulted in my mother, her three sisters and a brother being separated and going to live with different family members. My mother went to live in England when she was seventeen years of age and lived there until the early 1950s, when she came back to Ireland and married my father, Pat Henry. I feel that I have inherited my mother's assertiveness and intelligence, and I hope a little of her wonderful zest for life. As far back as I can remember she was always elegant, well dressed and well groomed. She learned to drive whilst she lived in England, and she was the first of her generation in our home locality to be able to do so. Pictures of my mother when she was young show her to be an incredibly beautiful woman, and she stayed this way her entire life, ageing remarkably well.

My father's personality was quite opposite to my mother in many ways. He was generally considered a contemplative man. Indeed, he was a quiet and reflective person, but he also maintained a very humorous side to his character which was frequently seen by those who knew him well. Father hated arguments and avoided conflict whenever he could. He was my grandparents' only son and grew up with seven sisters in tow. He told me a story when I was a young boy that I have never forgotten.

Once there was a man who went to England. Before he went he had heard stories about gold being found everywhere on the streets of London. As luck would have it, his dream seemed to come true! When he arrived in London, there before him were several coins on the street. However, he felt tired after his journey and felt too lazy to pick them up, so he decided to return the following day. This, he thought, would be the beginning of his good fortune. Now he could become a rich man with pockets overflowing with gold coins. But when he returned the next day, to his dismay, there was not a coin in sight! Day after day, week after week, he fruitlessly searched every street for more coins. His searching was relentless but sadly the result was always the same. In the end he didn't find a single coin, squashing his dreams forever.

My father was essentially a family man, and he enjoyed being a farmer, loving both his cattle and working on the land. He was a very devout Catholic who would pray on his knees every night before going to bed. He hated cheap things because he believed things that were cheap never last very long. Father never bought anything that was second-hand. Indeed, I grew up listening to his philosophy that 'the dearest is the cheapest in the long run'. He hated pubs and blamed alcohol for ruining people's lives and causing poverty, but he did like to smoke and used to enjoy his pipe every night. I was often dispatched to the local shop if he ran out of his beloved 'Murray's Plug Tobacco'. Father smoked cigarettes too but only after church on Sundays, when he could be seen smoking 'Players', his favourite brand.

My brother John followed in my father's footsteps and from an early age cultivated a deep interest in the land and farming. He was also intrigued with different types of machinery and articulated vehicles, learning to drive at a very young age. His other great passion was watching westerns on television, particularly the *High Chaparral*. I personally couldn't understand westerns and questioned why so many elderly men got shot dead at the slightest argument. It didn't make sense to me that they had lived such long lives to end up getting killed so easily and over something so trivial. It must have made sense to John because he seemed to love them. He later inherited my father's farm and went to work on the land as a full-time farmer.

My second oldest brother, Kevin, was a keen gardener and was very knowledgeable about all things horticultural. He designed and looked after the gardens at home and relished sowing various kinds of shrubs, flowers and vegetables in each plot. He knew the names of every plant and the individual characteristics of each type. Kevin took after my mother and loved reading, both classical and contemporary novels, and between the two of them we could have easily set up a small library at home.

I used to walk half a mile to meet Kevin on his way home from secondary school, as I was still in primary school at the time and would be home before him. The first thing I would ask upon meeting him was whether he had any post. Johnny Cone, our postman, who always dressed in his full uniform with peaked cap, used to give our letters and parcels to Kevin most mornings as he waited for the school bus at the end of our road. Johnny was getting old and coming up to retirement age. Giving the mail to Kevin saved him cycling a mile to our house to deliver it, but the disadvantage of this was that Kevin would have to take the mail to school with him. Most of the mail we got anyway was for either Kevin or me, as we were always sending off for new records. Our mother had bought us a record player and we used to order singles and LPs, which were invariably the latest releases from *Top of the Pops*, from catalogues like Carlin Records in County Down.

Kevin was also very good at home décor and regularly did the wallpapering and painting in our house. My mother preferred Kevin's work, as she claimed that father used to miss parts when painting. Admittedly, father wasn't the best with a paintbrush and gladly left this task to Kevin. Despite his love of gardening Kevin didn't pursue a career in horticulture, and after he left school he joined the police force.

Finally, there was my third brother, Padraic. People were always remarking on how handsome he was, which made me rather jealous because I wanted them to say similar things about me! However, whilst he surpassed me with good looks, he didn't manage to do the same in the height department. Padraic was the smallest of my brothers, and at five feet, seven inches cowered underneath the rest of us, who were all closer to six feet. But like John, he too was into mechanics and machinery and was very gifted in this area. Padraic smoked and drank, much to the disapproval of my parents, creating a lifestyle of late-night dances and parties, and because of his looks he was never short of female company. He had dark blond hair, which was quite different to the rest of us. John and Kevin had black and red hair respectively, and my hair was brown, or 'mouse-brown' as my siblings preferred to call it because they knew it would irritate me. After Padraic left school he went to serve an apprenticeship as a mechanic in a garage in Gurteen – a small village five miles from our home.

Gurteen was a delightfully tranquil place with two clothes shops, a big supermarket, a hardware shop, a few public houses, and even a chemist's. Mrs Johnston, the owner of the chemist's, was a recognised quack for curing ailments in both humans and animals to the extent that local people considered her superior to any doctor or vet. Say, for instance, a farmer went to her for advice on a sick calf suffering from scour, Mrs Johnston would produce a remedy which would cure it. Likewise, if the farmer complained that his gout was paining him, she would invariably be able to give him some medicine to alleviate his suffering as well.

The large secondary school provided Gurteen village with the energies of youth, whilst an entrepreneurial side of the village was evident in the large garage where Padraic worked. It was the focal point for purchasing new cars and farm machinery, and for bringing such vehicles for periodic servicing. Gurteen also had its own creamery, where farmers brought milk directly from their farms and in return bought farm manure and other agricultural necessities.

Padraic used to cycle to work every morning, but my mother often picked him up in the evening in our Ford Transit van, which my father bought around this time. Kevin and I usually accompanied her, as it was a novelty to go on these little trips. The road to Gurteen from our house was quiet, particularly in wintertime, with very few other vehicles on it after dusk. Try imagining travelling along a narrow country road for a few miles without any turnings and then, suddenly, coming to a bend where down in a hollow you see lights on the distant horizon. This was Gurteen – we nicknamed it 'The City of Lights'. It was a treat to see this sight on every trip, but the journey home was less enthralling as it nearly always entailed being huddled up in the back of the van with Padraic's bicycle. Later on, however, Padraic bought a motorbike and this unfortunately resulted in us making less frequent trips to Gurteen in the evening.

∽

There was major upheaval in our house in the early seventies when my parents had some extra rooms built at the back. A larger kitchen was one of the projects. This construction work meant lots of shifting things around for several months. Nevertheless, the excitement of going into these new rooms after they were completed was incredible. I remember looking at them in total wonderment – it was as if we had moved to another house. The building works included the new kitchen and bathroom, new water and heating system complete with radiators along with an exciting new back entrance to the house. Everything was novel and fresh and in that era had a really modern feel about it. We thought we were really grand, and to a certain degree we were.

My mother always took pride in maintaining the family home and, with the help of Kevin's decorating skills, she created something unique and special for all the family. We basically had a clean and well-maintained home both inside and out. Kevin's gardening abilities were evident in the presentation of the front garden with massive rows of lupins with their vivid colours of purple and yellow, roses, nasturtiums and chrysanthemums, all with their fragrant scents on display.

The extension to our house now meant that we had fresh drinking water coming straight from the taps. Previously, spring water had to be collected from a well a hundred yards from our home. My father maintained the well with great care, building small stone steps to lead down to it and then partially covering it over with bricks to prevent grass, dirt or leaves getting into the water. The well was not big but was certainly considered deep enough to drown in, so I was duly warned to stay clear of it when I was very young. However, being a typical child, the well prompted my curiosity to the extent that I was eventually allowed to go there either with my mother or one of my brothers and watch them scoop the spring water into a bucket.

Mother always lit a fire every day in mine and Kevin's bedroom during wintertime. I shared the bed with Kevin, and this proved problematic at times, especially in the middle of the night if the top sheet ended up around your neck when the blankets went askew. I often remember waiting wearily whilst the light was switched on and Kevin made the bed before any bit of comfort could be had. But it is lovely to recall those early days going to sleep as a young boy in a fire-lit room, as I watched the flames merrily glow while the heat coaxed me to sleep.

During the early seventies another change took place in Ireland that greatly affected us and indeed took quite a lot of getting used to. This was decimalisation and the introduction of a new currency – the punt making its debut. I had grown rather fond of the old penny coin, such a beautifully crafted coin with a hen and two of its chickens on the front. 'Pingin' was inscribed on it in Gaelic, meaning 'one penny'. The back of the coin had the traditional emblem of Ireland, a harp, with the word 'Eire' above it. Now these coins were being replaced by new ones, which, although new and shiny, were nevertheless not as interesting as their predecessors. Despite being a different currency from sterling, the new punt, which was of less value than sterling, shared the same denominations of coins and paper money. Therefore, into our midst came coinage of varying value from a halfpenny to a penny, then two pence, five pence, ten pence and fifty pence. The punt itself was in green paper notes.

Ireland was indeed a country that saw many changes in the early seventies. It was one of the poorest countries in Western Europe then with a declining population, poor living standards and weak economic prospects. Joining the European Union in 1973 brought a glimmer of hope to the country with the wish that it would benefit from some European funding to boost its economy and infrastructure.

Yet still the violence in Northern Ireland continued on a daily basis. The terrible events which took place there lacked a sense of reality to people living in the Republic, particularly those like my family and I who lived in rural parts of the west of Ireland. Growing up from an early age on a diet of watching and listening to daily bulletins of death, hatred and mayhem, I became almost desensitised to it all. We neither saw first-hand nor experienced any of the atrocities that were happening in Ulster. It was at times as if these brutalities were going on in some distant land and not in another part of Ireland, even though my family's home was geographically only sixty miles from Northern Ireland's border. But the first time I became really aware of the terrible events in Ulster was in 1972 when the awful pictures of Bloody Sunday became ingrained in people's minds in January of that year. The British Army shot dead thirteen unarmed civil rights protesters in cold blood during a demonstration in Derry and injured several others. This was the pivotal moment when the troubles in Northern Ireland reached an unimaginable state of crisis, especially after the inquiry into the murders resulted in no charges being brought against the soldiers who carried out this brutality.

A powerfully worded lyric written by John Lennon and Yoko Ono sums up the anger shared by many about Bloody Sunday:

> Well it was Sunday bloody Sunday
> When they shot the people there
> The cries of thirteen martyrs
> Filled the free Derry air
> Is there any one amongst you?
> Dare to blame it on the kids?
> Not a soldier boy was bleeding
> When they nailed the coffin lids.

Ireland became stigmatised as a people because our nationality was linked throughout the world to the Provisional Irish Republican Army and terrorism. This often brought a demeanour of apology simply for being Irish. Foreigners invariably considered the troubles of Northern Ireland to include the Republic and were always surprised to discover the peacefulness of our country when they visited the South. Most people in rural Ireland spoke very little about the Provisional IRA and didn't know anybody who was directly or indirectly involved in it, but remarked on its senseless shootings and bombings. There were, however, a few elderly men from neighbouring villages who belonged to the Old IRA, which predated the Provisional IRA. These elderly men were sympathetic to the views of republicanism, and had at one stage been active volunteers. Their involvement predominantly came to light at their funerals. I attended such funerals as a young boy with my parents and used to think how grand it was that their coffins were draped in the national flag of Ireland – the tricolour with its distinctive green, white and gold colours. But apart from the flag adorning their coffins, the priests would make no mention of their IRA involvement during the funeral Masses. The reason for this was a combination of denial and a fear of saying anything that could be misconstrued or cause embarrassment. Therefore, priests, or at least those in our parish, kept firmly to the traditional Catholic funeral ritual and treated Old IRA 'soldiers' with the same reverence as any other ordinary deceased person. Afterwards, in the cemetery, a volley of three shots from a rifle would be fired over the dead man's grave, after the final prayers had been recited and the priest had left of course, to signify the contribution the deceased had made to gaining freedom for Ireland.

The Old IRA was descended from the formation of the Irish Republic in 1922. This event was directly linked to the Easter Rising of 1916, which paved the way for the formation of an Irish government to rule over twenty-six of Ireland's thirty-two counties, separating the new Republic from British rule. But before this was possible, Ireland was made to endure the wrath of British rule for one last time. The Black and Tans, nicknamed after their mismatched uniforms, consisted of 8,000 former English soldiers sent by Whitehall to assist the Royal Irish Constabulary in the policing of rural Ireland in 1920. Their goal was to cleanse Ireland of Republican rebels, but in doing so they grossly misused their authority and terrorised Irish families at every opportunity, becoming notorious for burning and looting the homes of ordinary countryside civilians. Thankfully, the outcry at their brutality meant they only stayed a year.

Several Old IRA members fought and lost their lives to give Ireland the freedom to become a Republic with its own government. But they were still dissatisfied that six of Ulster's nine counties remained under British rule. Members of the Old IRA were becoming elderly by the late 1960s, with most of them in their late seventies or early eighties. Hence, it became a matter of 'out with the old and in with the new', and the new Provisional IRA was formed with the same purpose as the Old IRA: to seek ways of getting rid of the British occupation of Northern Ireland. Sadly, the Provisional IRA thought the best way to achieve this goal would be by violence, and at every opportunity incited mayhem and brutality in the hope of achieving a united Ireland. The vision was for an Ireland totally free from British control and having full authority over the thirty-two counties for the first time in centuries.

An old rebel song that was sometimes played on the radio when I was a child amused me, if only for the forlorn tone of its verse. The song, of unknown origin, was entitled *Old Ireland Free Once More*. Back then I knew little, and cared even less, about Ireland's freedom or the oppression that some Irish citizens felt we were under. But nevertheless the words *'Oh Gra mo chree* (meaning the love of my heart), *I long to see old Ireland free once more,'* brought a smile to my face whenever I heard them sung. Little did I realise then that life in the west of Ireland under this 'assumed captivity' was a thousand times more idyllic than life in Northern Ireland, where the IRA fought so vigorously for an 'idealistic freedom' through their daily warfare and extreme violence.

> Last night I had a happy dream,
> though restless where I be
> I dreamt again, brave Irishmen
> had set old Ireland free
> And how excited I became
> when I heard the cannons roar
> Oh Gra mo chree, I long to see
> Old Ireland free once more.
>
> It's true we've had brave Irishmen
> as everyone must know
> O'Neil, O'Donnell, Sarsfield too
> Lord Edward and Wolfe Tone

Also Robert Emmett
Who till death did not give o'er
Oh Gra mo chree, I long to see
Old Ireland free once more.

Now we can't forget the former years
They're kept in memory still
Of the Wexford men of '98
Who fought on Vinegar Hill
With Father Murphy at their side
And the green flag waving o'er
Oh Gra mo chree, I long to see
Old Ireland free once more.

Allan, O'Brien and Larkin died
Their country to set free
Someday soon brave Irish men
Will make the English flee
By day and night they'll always fight
'Til death they'll not give o'er
Oh Gra mo chree, I long to see
Old Ireland free once more.

2

Rural Happenings

My father's farm was primarily a beef farm, meaning that his herd of livestock were Hereford, Aberdeen Angus, Charolais and Limousin bullocks. He kept some Friesian cows too, but these only supplied milk for our own family use. We also had a pony called Kitty and a donkey called Bess, as well as some pigs. I grew up helping my father vaccinate cattle against diseases such as black leg and red water, and I often tended to sick animals, particularly young calves that fell ill with scour. I fetched buckets of water and patted their brows in the hope of easing their discomfort. I helped clean out barns, fed hay to the cattle and from an early age became no stranger to farmyard smells like Jeyes Fluid, creosote, fertilizer and weed killer.

All the fields on the farm had different names, some obvious and some less so. For example, our pigs spent most of their outdoor life in a field behind the sty; hence, it was referred to as the 'sow's field'. Then there was the limekiln field, which had a hump in its middle. My grandfather used to extract lime from this field and occasionally sold some of it. Some other fields acquired the nickname 'Georgies' named after the previous owner. Indeed, every field on the farm held its own particular story.

The best part of growing up on a farm was the outdoor freedom it gave. This was particularly true for me in the 1970s when it came to summer and the annual haymaking. The Irish climate made this a particularly tricky time. Ideally, hay was made in late June and early July, but more often than not, due to the unpredictable weather, this task spilled over into late July and August.

Summer really was all about haymaking; there was no escaping it on the farm and when the weather was right, the pleasure gained from this activity could be anticipated. There was nothing more beautiful than sitting in the shade on a glorious day in a hayfield in the middle of summer whilst picnicking on sandwiches, cake and tea. There was something so truly special about its simplicity that is difficult to explain to those who have never experienced it.

Turning the day-old cut hay with a pitchfork was very boring, and putting it into 'laps' – small gatherings – was equally monotonous. My favourite part of the haymaking process was placing it into small stacks. These larger gatherings of hay were then colloquially referred to as 'cocks of hay'. It was at this stage that the haymaking process began to liven up. Looking back I believe my neat habits of today must somehow originate from those days. When my father was making haycocks, I would rake around the immediate area and ensure that all the hay was neatly gathered up. My father hated mess, so I tried not to miss any bits. Then I would help him make a hay rope to put on the haycock. This entailed me rotating the hayrack at the same time as my father spun hay in order to make the rope. My father bought a lot of new hay-making machinery in the early seventies, and John and Padraic were particularly good at using the new mower, haymaker and cock-lifter. These new machines really sped things up on the farm, especially as time was of the essence owing to the unpredictable climate.

We had the most adorable dog imaginable on the farm. His name was Captain, a beautiful black and white collie dog with brown paws and the occasional brown spot on his face. Everywhere I was, he was, and vice versa. He was a big part of my life throughout my teenage years and contributed greatly to the enchantment of growing up on a farm. One summer when Padraic was driving the tractor and cutting the meadow in the 'bank fields', he didn't see Captain, who was lurk-ing for frogs in the grass, and ran into him, the mower slicing off a piece of his front left paw. I was terribly upset and feared he would die. His paw looked terrible and he was in a lot of pain – he just continu-ally licked the open wound. Thankfully, Kevin was able to get some medicine from the vet. It was a white powder that we had to mix with milk. A week passed before he showed any signs of recovery. His paw eventually healed up, leaving a big gash, but this didn't seem to hinder his mobility.

The hardest part of haymaking, which generally needed a lot of strength, was trampling the hay in the hayshed when it was brought home from the fields. Either my father or John would use a pitchfork to lift the hay up to Kevin and myself and onto the bed of hay. We in turn would fork it to the back and sides of the shed and trample it down with our feet, which was physically very tiring work. Padraic was fast with the tractor and would quickly make the journey to and from the fields with the cocks of hay on the cock-lifter, and there was seldom any time to rest in-between, but when there was I would call Captain, who would come running towards the shed. He was the best dog ever at climbing ladders and he would quickly ascend up onto the hay bed. I had to carry him down the ladder though because he couldn't manage by himself, and it was way too far for him to jump.

It was always a relief and a joy to hear mother's voice call out 'How are ye getting on?' because when you heard this, you automatically knew it was time for dinner or tea, and you also knew she had prepared something nice. My mother was a terrific cook, and there was nothing she couldn't turn her hand to when it came to preparing food. She also always managed to bake the most delicious soda bread and delicacies like apple tarts, scones and fruitcake.

We were fortunate at home to have plenty of apple trees in a small orchard, which bore a good quantity of fruit each year. However, the apples usually tasted very bitter, so mother used them for baking apple tarts. We had a big plum tree as well, which also yielded a great crop of fruit. Furthermore, father rooted rhubarb plants as well as looking after the fruit trees by making sure they were pruned each spring.

Another feature of summertime was the saving of turf on the peat bog. This was as big a task as gathering the hay but slightly less reliant on the unpredictable Irish climate. Every household saved turf, and this peat was the main fuel used for heating homes in the west of Ireland as few homes had central heating at that time. The village of Derrykinlough became an entrepreneurial place for the production of turf, and there was a company called 'Morgan and Burke', owned by Denis Lee – a Sligo businessman. Denis built a large workshop on a

BURIED DEEP IN MY HEART

small piece of land that my father sold to him especially for this purpose. This workshop, known locally as 'The Hut', was used to repair all types of machinery, including the two turf-cutting machines and the tractors used for work on the bog during the turf-cutting season, which ran from April to September each year. I would estimate that the company employed over a hundred different people over the two decades when it was at its peak, and teenagers came every year during the summer holiday for part-time work. It was lovely growing up in the village at this time because there were always so many people about, adding a flavour of excitement.

Whilst Derrykinlough was buzzing with energy and excitement every summer, I must be frank and admit that I found saving turf quite a laborious affair. Firstly, the turf had to be given enough time to dry out after it was cut. Then it had to be turned over and broken into small pieces. After another week or two, when the turf was reasonably dry, it was 'footed', which meant putting it into small piles to allow more air to get underneath for it to dry faster. After a few more weeks it was put into 'clamps', which were larger gatherings. Finally, it had to be brought home from the bog and neatly put into the turf shed. After the turf shed was full, father would build a 'reek' with the remaining turf. A 'reek' was similar in design to a clamp but much larger at three and a half metres high and twelve metres long. Father's reeks were always neat in their construction and after one was built it would be covered with plastic sheeting to shield it from the harsh climate. But the hard work was worth it, especially in wintertime, with my parents taking pride in always having fine glowing turf fires in our home, keeping it friendly and warm.

I must tell you about Brian, a young man who came to work on the bog one summer. His lovely and endearing personality furthered my awakening to knowing what lovely people life can produce. I was about ten at the time and he was about sixteen or seventeen – perhaps a little younger. Tall, lanky and with a cheerful laugh he was the life and soul of the place. Youth and a totally uncomplicated attitude to life were his. Brian cycled five miles every day from his home to

Derrykinlough, where he turned and footed turf and helped to fill tractors with it. He was seen riding his bike to and fro around the village and his presence became so normal that it was hard to imagine the place without him. Brian was always nice and friendly towards me because he knew all of my family and would often drop in to visit and have a laugh about something or other. He was simply a delight to be around and to have around. Brian was also a good singer, and one of his favourite songs to sing was *Spancil Hill*. This is a well-known Irish ballad dating back to the 1870s about a hill between the towns of Ennis and Tulla in County Clare. Many Irish singers have recorded this song through the years, including the renowned folk group The Wolfe Tones. The song has a very amusing rhyme to it:

Last night as I lay dreaming
Of pleasant days gone by
Me mind being bent on travelling
To Ireland I did fly
I stepped aboard a vision
And followed with my will
Until next I came to anchor
At the cross near Spancil Hill

Delighted by the novelty
Enchanted with the scene
Where in my early boyhood
Where often I had been
I thought I heard a murmur
And think I hear it still
It's the little stream of water
That flows down Spancil Hill

It being the 23rd of June
The day before the fair
Where Ireland's sons and daughters
In crowds assembled there
The young, the old, the brave and the bold
They came for sport and kill
There were jovial conversations
At the cross near Spancil Hill

I went to see my neighbours
To hear what they might say
The old ones were all dead and gone
The others turning grey
I met with tailor Quigley
He's as bald as ever still
Sure he used to make my britches
When I lived in Spancil Hill

I paid a flying visit
To my first and only love
She's white as any lily
And gentle as a dove
She threw her arms around me
Saying Johnny I love you still
She's Meg the farmer's daughter
And the pride of Spancil Hill

I dreamt I stooped and kissed her
As in the day of 'ore
She said Johnny you're only joking
As many the times before
The cock crew in the morning
He crew both loud and shrill
And I woke in California
Many miles from Spancil Hill

I recall two other activities taking place each September. The first was the harvesting of the fields of oats that father sowed each springtime. Oats were commonly used on Irish farms as a supplement to livestock feed. Unlike hay, their cultivation wasn't as reliant on having a good summer, and neither did the harvesting require the same amount of attention as haymaking. The oat leaves were cut about four inches above ground level, and after being cut, the leaves would be put into shocks. I loved the smell of oats and often burst open a plant just to taste the seeds. The shocks were left in the field for a short period before being ready to take home to be stored in a barn.

Father also sowed potatoes in early summer, and these would be ready to uproot each September. He would dig them up from the side of the ridge with a spade to avoid damaging any, whilst I would pull out the potato stalk. It was exciting to discover how many potatoes would reveal themselves after a stalk was pulled – would I be able to count six, eight or ten potatoes? Each stalk would have potatoes of varying sizes hanging off them, and the larger ones had to be kept separate from the smaller ones. A really small potato was given the nickname *poirín* – an old Irish name for something small and useless. The harvesting of potatoes was also very humbling considering how much our Irish ancestors had depended on this vegetable as their main source of sustenance in bygone days.

My father went to England every autumn for economic reasons to work in a sugar factory in Essex. Thus, he was usually away from September to early February. His annual absence had become part of our family life, and we were used to it. We were sad at his departure but excited when he returned. Father always ensured that affairs on the farm were in order before he left, including getting all the hay and turf home. All that remained was for my brothers and I to help mother run the farm whilst he was away, which mainly meant milking cows, feeding cattle and cleaning out barns. Selling and buying cattle was always done in spring, but my father always returned in time for this task. However, the calving season was mainly in wintertime, and it was at these times that I had to get my hands really dirty. No two births were ever the same. With difficult births, the cows went through immense pain, and plenty of assistance had to be given when big calves were involved. For this, a rope was tied around the front feet of the calf after the water bag had broken, and a strong piece of wood was then attached to the rope to assist with pulling the calf out as quickly as possible. As soon as the calf was born, I used to help clean and dry it off with some hay. It never ceased to amaze me how after the young calf was dried off and had rested a little, it would then rise to its feet. This always happened within minutes and was truly magical to watch.

My mother used to pack my father's suitcase meticulously before he went to England, and she usually had an audience when carrying out this task, as I liked to watch what she was putting in. Everything put into the suitcase had been washed and meticulously ironed – so it didn't matter that his work clothes were mixed in with his best finery. A quantity of razor blades, soap and shampoo intended to last him for a couple of months were also included. As a letter was the main means of correspondence in those days, she always included a blue Belvedere Bond notepad and envelopes to match. My mother and I exchanged letters with father every week with our news, and to this day I vividly remember his address at the sugar factory in Essex.

Mr Patrick Henry,
The Hostel,
Felsted Sugar Factory,
Dunmow,
Essex,
England.

In addition to writing to us, father regularly posted us newspapers. This was a treat because we all loved reading in our house, and the newspapers he sent were different from the Irish ones with a wider variety of stories which weren't normally available to us. Indeed, part of my literary diet growing up were *Daily Mirror* newspapers, which father carefully rolled up and posted to us. There was nothing better than getting a taste for scandal from an early age. It was all very harmless, though mind-boggling at the time. In the midst of a staunch Catholic environment, reading about an adulterer was shocking! Questions like 'How could they do such a thing?' would often be exchanged in conversations. It wasn't only reading about the sexual antics of people that was intriguing, other stories struck a chord as well.

For me, my Catholic upbringing encouraged a fascination with the afterlife and the supernatural. I was always asking what happened to people after they died. I really wanted to see a ghost, but I never did. Maybe it was just as well because I remember reading in one of the papers a really scary story about a haunted house. Furniture often

26

moved around by itself in this house, noises were often heard in the middle of the night, and a misty, cold presence was sometimes felt in its rooms. Well, nothing moved in our house, wardrobes stayed firmly in their place at all times, and neither were there any strange sightings. I know because I did a daily check after reading this real-life ghost story. Furthermore, if the kitchen or sitting room were cold, it was usually the fault of one of my brothers or me for neglecting to fuel the fire whilst my mother was out working on the farm.

My father always brought us presents when he came home each spring. One year he brought me a lovely Parker pen. I loved it, but my mother gave strict instructions that I shouldn't take it to school for fear it would be lost or stolen.

The excitement of father coming home was coupled one year by the arrival of a travelling show to our local area. I have realised over the years that individuals can be rather naïve during many stages in their lives, but none more so than the young and impressionable. It is when you are young that only true wonderment can be experienced. I remember feeling this sense of wonder when the travelling show came to a neighbouring village. The anticipation of what the shows were going to be like was immense. A marquee was erected in a field at the back of the church, but there was only a small entourage with just three or four caravans for the family-run business.

Shows were planned over the course of a week and were mainly scheduled for seven o'clock each evening. I remember entering the marquee on the first evening and being taken aback and fascinated by the lighting as we sat down on one of the rows of benches. The performance was an all-round show for all ages and consisted of a comedy act, magic tricks, singing, and even a trapeze artist. Then to finish things off at the end of what was a lovely and enjoyable evening there was a round of bingo with prizes to be won which consisted of a teddy bear, a crystal bowl or a box of biscuits. However, I wasn't fortunate enough to win anything and envied those who did.

Each evening there was a horror movie shown at either ten or eleven o'clock, but this was too late for me to be allowed to attend. I remember my curiosity about these movies and would have loved to see the gore that I imagined. Padraic went to some of them though and was questioned thoroughly about them. He was asked questions like 'What was it about?' and 'Who was in it?' as well as 'What did you see?' I don't think he was very interested in them because he could never really remember much about the storyline, which I found rather infuriating at the time.

Ireland had begun to reap some benefits of being part of the European Market by this time. Nearly every household now had a car, there were better employment prospects, and women were entering the workforce in much larger numbers. More cars and more money meant that people were able to travel much longer distances in search of entertainment. As a result, people began to develop broader minds and more sophisticated tastes. The tourism industry saw an increase in the number of visitors coming to Ireland, alongside emigrants returning home on vacation, all of which generated ever more income. I missed the travelling show after it left, and it was never to return again. It was the last of its kind; society had changed. It was the end of an era and simplistic shows like these couldn't survive the new economic boom.

My mother grew up in the village of Brackloon, which was situated three miles away from Derrykinlough, and she inherited her grandmother and uncle's cottage and farm when they passed away. Brackloon wasn't a big village and there were only about half a dozen dwellings in it, but it became a sort of home from home for me. Visiting the village took up a lot of my time during my youth. I would cycle there at least three times a week, through rain or sunshine, to count father's cattle in case any of them had broken a fence and strayed into neighbouring fields or onto the main road. Brackloon was also much frequented in summertime for haymaking. It always felt like going on an excursion for this, as we packed food and drinks to last for most of the day. There was even a big hayshed there for the new hay to be trampled.

A trip to Brackloon usually entailed popping in to see Nora, my father's cousin. She was an elderly woman, well into her eighties, who lived in a neat thatched cottage, and I frequently visited her during my regular trips to Brackloon. She had a great affection for my father, and, despite the distant relationship, considered all of my family as part of her 'family'. We maintained this link through Nora's sister in Ballymote, whom I mentioned in an earlier chapter. Nora was unmarried and shared our surname. She had spent much of her earlier life in America before returning home to live in Ireland, and my father always called her 'Hanora', which always made her laugh.

I can't recall a time when I ever saw Nora's front door closed. When I called to visit I would always find her sitting next to an open fire in her kitchen. She would look up when she heard my knock on the door and smile broadly, her hand signalling for me to sit in the chair opposite her. She loved people coming to see her and never appeared unprepared when visitors dropped in unexpectedly. The conversation was always light-hearted and usually consisted of news about happenings within the family or about school affairs. As well as being a gracious old lady she was a generous one too and often gave me money during a visit. Nora's two-roomed thatched cottage was whitewashed outside and had a bright red door. But there was something else that really stood out about her home. Her kitchen also served as her living room and bedroom. Nora's cottage was very old-fashioned in the sense that the kitchen had a bed, partitioned off by curtains, located in a corner near the open fireplace. Imagine how warm and cosy it must have been in the wintertime. Nora had a large dresser laid with Delph of every description, including her best blue willow patterned tea set. Undoubtedly her dresser also contained many family heirlooms she had inherited from her parents and grandparents. Nora's cottage was such an enchanting little place to visit, and I loved going there to see her. She passed away a few years later at the grand age of ninety-three.

My father kept his cattle in two places on the land in Brackloon. Some were kept in the fields of 'Lugmore', referred to as 'Lug' for short. These fields could only be accessed via a boreen – with umpteen twists and turns. Lug was about three-quarters of a mile from the main road, and I would either walk or cycle to the fields to check and count the cattle for my father. The other cattle we had in Brackloon grazed in the fields at the back of the cottage. At the bottom of the fields was a river, which was fenced to stop the cattle straying into it and drowning.

A lady named Marie, who was in her fifties, rented mother's cottage in Brackloon, and she became a close family friend. From the time she came into our lives in 1973 up until her untimely death from cancer some years later, Marie played a central role not only in my life but also in the lives of all my family. As well as being a generous, kind and loving person, Marie was very discreet. I trusted her implicitly and confided in her about the arguments and everyday disputes that went on in the Henry family. She was like a second mother to me, and while growing up I relied on her for support, which she gave in abundance.

My friendship with Marie developed almost by accident. One autumn evening in 1974, a young calf went missing from one of the fields in Brackloon. I was eleven at the time, and I went with my father and two of my brothers to look for it. Our initial foray was fruitless so my father decided to extend the search. In what appeared to take ages, but was perhaps less than an hour, we searched behind the bushes and brambles in every field, as well as a stream or two along the way, but there was no calf to be found. Then we walked down to the river at the back of the fields. This, too, was unsuccessful, but the possibility remained that the calf had gone into the river and drowned, although this was thought to be unlikely.

The search eventually ground to a halt because we were running out of places to look. I got bored of searching for the calf. Father got fed up with my whining and asked me to go and wait in Marie's house whilst my brothers and he went further afield in search of the missing beast.

Though not a shy child at home, I was a little more bashful outside the family circle, and so I was quite apprehensive about this. I remember being rather nervous about going up to the back door to ask if I could come in and wait whilst the search for the calf continued. I need not have worried, for soon Marie and I got chatting about school and various other topics, and I soon became completely at ease as I drank tea and ate cake. The calf was eventually found late that evening, just as it was getting dark, under some gorse, which had evidently been overlooked earlier in the search.

I will always remember Marie's cottage for its simplicity and beauty. There was one room in particular that stood out – the kitchen, which also doubled as a living room. The layout of the house and kitchen was not unusual for a 1920s design, as in those days the kitchens were designed to be the central room of the house as well as acting as a thoroughfare. Thus the kitchen could be accessed from both front and back doors. Bedrooms were attached to the kitchen, usually with one on each side.

I can vividly recall those wonderful occasions, sitting in one of the armchairs next to the open fire in the kitchen while Marie made tea and buttered some of her home-baked loaf. She cooked all her bread on the open fire and had the most impressive technique of manoeuvring the crane over the open flames without getting burned or scalded when she did her baking. I always sat on the right-hand side of the fireplace because it was warm sitting next to the glowing fire. But there was another reason why this seating arrangement became habitual. When Marie's front door was open, I had discovered that a picture hanging over her large kitchen cabinet gave a perfect reflection in its glass of her beautiful flower garden outside. I loved looking at this picture. There was a big castle in the background and a young boy fishing on the bank of a river with a sailing boat close by.

There were several other striking characteristics to Marie's kitchen. It had a very large fireplace with a tall mantelpiece, and on the top of the mantelpiece were two big china dogs, one on each end, with a large clock in the centre. The floor had no covering on it, but it did not give the impression of bareness. Marie took great pride in her floor and ensured that she scrubbed the cement surface daily, which guaranteed that it was always clean. The décor of the room, with its light green paint and brown doors, contrasted with the cleanliness of the floor. The only other furniture in the kitchen, apart from what I have already described, was a gas cooker and a fridge.

There was also an intriguing alcove attached to Marie's kitchen. This was a little annexe where there was no light, and here Marie stored fuel for the fire as well as some other non-perishable goods. I never dared go into the alcove because of the darkness, but I always took a peep inside to see if its little door was open.

Before leaving Marie's kitchen, I must mention one last thing. This is the picturesque view one got when one stood at the back door looking towards a pathway leading down to the hayshed and vegetable garden. At its edges were rows and rows of pink bushes* for which nobody ever knew the correct name. The best way I can describe their appearance is a cross between fuchsias and rhododendrons. Not only was the sight exceedingly pretty when their blooms were full in late spring, but they also gave out an intoxicatingly pleasant basil scent.

There never seemed to be a dull moment in our house, there was always something happening to intrigue, amuse or cause vexation. I nearly forgot to mention my father's shotgun, which he kept in a corner of the kitchen. Nobody else dared touch or go near the gun, for if they did, they risked a severe reprimand from father, who was always incredibly careful not to leave the gun loaded and kept the cartridges under lock and key. He used this gun mainly to shoot or frighten crows or magpies that interfered with the vegetable garden or oat crops. Sometimes I saved these creatures of prey from a horrible end by cre-

---

* Pink bushes. The Royal Botanic Gardens at Kew have identified the plant I referred to as *heuchera*, an evergreen perennial herb, with graceful flowering spikes in subtle shades of coral pink during springtime.

ating a scarecrow or 'fear breaga' as it was called in Irish. I did this by cutting out cardboard from the back of a cornflake box and drawing a face. Then my mother would give me one of her old cardigans, which I would hang on a cross made from two thick sticks with a nail holding them together in the middle.

Every home in the countryside made butter from its farm, and I always compared drinking buttermilk to poison because of its bitter taste. It was a choice of either rushing to the nearest sink to spit it out or allowing the muscles of my face to squirm in horror as it was being swallowed.

My mother regularly made butter at home. This entailed collecting the cream from the fresh milk for several days beforehand then putting it in a glass churn. On the lid of the churn was a round ball designed for resting the left hand while the right hand spun the spinning handle, also attached to the lid. Turning the handle required great speed and perseverance in order to move the propellers around to separate the butter from the cream. After spinning for about ten minutes, butter would form on the top of the cream. This would then be scooped up, squeezed free of any remaining deposits of milk and put in a bowl. A spoon and knife helped to mould the new butter into shape before it was sprinkled with salt, which was added as a preservative. I think mother might have been too generous with the salt because I hated homemade butter on bread because of the salty taste. There were two other uses for buttermilk; it was either used as an ingredient for baking bread or given to the pigs on the farm, who enjoyed this treat immensely. It was a shame that I never got as much satisfaction from it as the pigs. In fact, whenever I saw the churn being taken out, I generally left the kitchen and got as far away as possible.

Old Irish myths and customs sometimes come with interesting snippets of wisdom picked up from previous generations; none more so than my father holding the belief that boiled Guinness was great for curing a cold. Indeed, he firmly preferred this remedy to anything else and used to boil a bottle of Guinness in a saucepan on the range cooker. Sometimes he would make this nightcap in wintertime irrespective of whether he had a cold or not! This concoction was also rumoured to be a great tonic if you were feeling rundown. I couldn't let my father prepare his brew without asking for a taste – there would have been no fun in just watching, the curiosity would have got the better of me sooner rather than later. The Guinness would take about ten minutes to boil on the range, then my father sweetened it with sugar, and I sometimes requested that he put in an extra spoonful to make it sweeter. He would then pour a small amount into a cup for me. It tasted really lovely, and I somehow imagined the smell of the Guinness to have changed once it was heated. Whatever the experience did for me, it didn't turn me into a lifelong drinker of the stuff. Despite enjoying tastes of it from my father on those cold winter nights in the 1970s, I have rarely drunk it since.

My father was also a great believer in taking cod-liver oil and I'm afraid he inflicted the belief on his offspring that taking it would prevent winter colds. Therefore, unlike the sampling of the boiled Guinness, I had no choice but to digest father's spoonful of this foul mixture every morning. I hated it to start with, but over time I grew not to be so disgusted and became immune to its bland oily taste without the urge to heave. I much preferred the myth that 'an apple a day keeps the doctor away' or the more humorous suggestion that followed this initial line 'an orange a day keeps everyone away!' I think we probably added on this limerick in our house about the orange, but I can't say so for sure!

Living in the west of Ireland brought with it the experience of hearing some rare sounds and rhythms of endangered wildlife, particularly the curlew and the corncrake. The corncrake is a shy and secretive bird that mainly comes to prominence in Derrykinlough in summer during the mating season. Being nocturnal, it is seldom seen, but those who have seen it hiding in meadows describe it as having a proud deportment because it always stands with its head slightly tilted back. But whilst rarely seen, few could say that they have never heard its distinctively haunting 'kerrx-kerrx' voice sometime or other between dusk and dawn. Its bewildering voice has often been compared to 'two notched sticks being rubbed together'. The curlew on the other hand is renowned for making its nest mainly in peat land. These medium-sized birds are brown in colour and have a distinctive long down-curved bill, which I imagine is rather useful for catching their favourite food – worms. Curlews love to entertain with a crescendo of notes that sound like 'coooo-leeee', as if they are trying to pronounce their name. However, I always thought their voice resembled a resonance of 'Where are you?' giving it a lost and lonesome echo.

3

St Joseph's

St Joseph's National School in Rooskey, County Mayo, was two and a half miles from my home, and passing through Rooskey on the bus seemed like going through a small town without shops or public houses. I feel that during one's youth one always takes on a distorted image of places, either imagining them to be bigger or smaller than they actually are. Rooskey was generally recognised as a built-up village in the sense that it had a lot of houses close to one another, although I am only talking about a dozen or so. I was used to the tranquillity of no one living near our house for a mile either side, so I imagined Rooskey to be larger than it actually was.

There was a bend in the road just before arriving at the front of the school, and on one side of this, a large pump provided spring water to the residents of the village. It was fairly unique because it was the only one of its kind in the locality. Therefore, I was always intrigued to see how it worked and would watch whenever I saw someone using it. It had a long lever, which had to be tugged downwards for the water to gush out. I generally held a fear of rivers and seas which stemmed back to my earlier childhood when I nearly drown. Apparently, one day I was playing with my brothers in one of the fields when I fell into a small stream nearby, prompting them to swiftly rescue me from diaster. Although, I remembered little of the incident, it left me nervous of water, to the point I was apprehensive at the speed of it coming out of the pump.

Unlike many people whose memories of their first day at school are clear in their minds, mine are quite dim. I can vaguely recall the preparations when I was taken to town for new clothes, shoes and a school bag. However, I do remember people saying how lucky I was to be able to go to school by minibus. Moreover, I was considered to be in the lap of luxury by travelling to school in a minibus that picked me up directly from the front door and dropped me off outside the school gates. None of my brothers had this service and either had to walk or cycle to school.

When I first started at St Joseph's, the classroom desks still had inbuilt inkwells. Pupils used old-fashioned ink and quill pens, which had to be dipped into the inkwell regularly. We probably looked a little like characters from an updated version of a Charles Dickens novel. There was a certain skill in using the pen, which I'm afraid I never quite fully mastered. The process had to be done slowly because if one rushed it, ink would leak out, leaving an almighty big blob on the exercise page. Alas, this happened to me more often than not. The teacher would get incredibly angry with me, and I would be blamed for destroying a page of work, albeit unintentionally.

A young woman by the name of Mary O'Toole drove the school minibus. She was in her early twenties, and all my friends and I were very fond of her. She had a nice bubbly personality and interacted very well with young people. As she was chatty, her natural warmth encouraged us to confide all our school secrets to her. However, I often became embarrassed when friends told Mary about misdemeanours from class, especially if they divulged that a teacher had scolded me for misbehaving. But there were some misdemeanours that were unrepeatable, and nobody ever mentioned any of the punishments handed out by the brutal headmaster, who instilled an atmosphere of fear and trepidation into all our lives.

McGuire, the headmaster, had been ill intermittently for some months, and we had grown accustomed to him missing days off school. In fact, there were days when we almost became complacent and took it for granted that he wouldn't be coming in. However, this false sense of security was shattered when he got better and started turning up every day again. His manner was equally threatening and abusive after he returned, and he seemed determined to live up to his hard reputation until the point of his retirement.

Almost everything about McGuire was brown – brown trousers, brown jacket, brown shoes and brown tie. And then there was even the brown Ford Cortina. I remember the despair I often felt when Miss Driscoll, the junior teacher, would help us with our homework before he arrived. Even she was frightened of him and knew that if we hadn't done the homework in a certain way, he would get angry and physically assault us in return. Although her help was much appreciated, it wasn't always enough. How my heart would plunge when I would see his car pull up by the school gates, knowing that time had run out and that I would have to face him with incomplete homework.

One day I was made to go up to his desk and recite a poem from my English book. I can't recall the exact piece of work, but I remember it was a poem about February. He looked over his spectacles, and I instantly knew by his glare that he wasn't pleased with my efforts. I was asked to repeat the poem, which I did. He glared once more, and I knew by the way he cleared his throat that I was in trouble.

'You stupid idiot … Pronounce "February". Did you hear me? Pronounce "February" correctly,' he shouted.

Apparently I wasn't pronouncing the 'r' in the middle of the word 'February', and he made me repeat it time after time. The more I repeated it the more I became anxious and confused. My mind was a blank, and I couldn't try any harder. I wasn't getting it right and his anger was intensifying. He started to rise up from his seat, and this could only mean one thing. He didn't have to threaten. He knew that I would understand the signal, which meant he was either going to slap me across the face or kick me from behind.

Did he really see who was standing before him? I was just ten at the time, and there I was standing with my back to the rest of the class yet conscious of their presence. I can even remember my clothes. I was dressed in a grey pullover and blue shirt, my tall skinny frame frozen as I anticipated the next few minutes. If I could have seen my own face, I would have imagined it to be ghostly white with the pupils of my eyes enlarged. But my expression would have been stoic because I knew that he loathed children he considered to be weak. There would have been no pleas for mercy because experience had taught us that if you pleaded for him not to hit you, the beating would be doubled. Crying was also off limits because he hated boys showing this type of emotion and would have ridiculed me for doing so.

Then something surreal happened. It was as if someone had got inside my head and made me pronounce 'February' in the way that he wanted it. I hadn't noticed that I had said it any differently, so I couldn't understand how I had been mispronouncing it before. He simply muttered something indicating that I had pronounced it correctly and then sat down again.

And so I was saved from a beating, or saved on this occasion at least, but I knew there would be other occasions before the year came to an end. I waited in dread for these other times whilst counting the days to the summer holidays and his impending retirement. But McGuire appeared to become more psychotic in the weeks leading up to his departure. I have a faded memory of him getting all the boys in the school to march up and down in the schoolyard in a military-style parade one lunchtime. What the purpose of this was or whether he had some sort of grand illusion of himself being a sergeant major and we his soldiers is anyone's guess. It is difficult to figure out a personality as disordered as his appeared to be. We had no option but to do as we were told, so we did the drills – left, right, left, right whilst alternative arms swayed in motion to the marching – in order to satisfy a madman who relished in holding us in his power.

The summer holidays finally arrived, and so too did his retirement. As he had been headmaster for over twenty-five years, his deputy wrote to all the parents requesting donations to buy him a leaving present. There was a party on his last day, but it wasn't customary for parents to attend such events as farmers and their wives were considered too busy to break off from their work in the middle of the day for social gatherings of this kind. On this occasion they didn't miss any excitement because there simply wasn't any. Apart from the pupils of the school, McGuire and Miss Driscoll, the only other guest was the parish priest. The priest's task was to present him with the gift of crystal tumblers with a matching decanter and to make a speech. I can still see McGuire's fake smile when the gift was presented to him – he didn't deserve it, we deserved better. Maybe I didn't think it then, but I have thought it since, here were young children sipping orange squash, eating cake and biscuits whilst watching a monster receive a nice present. He should never have been a teacher because he didn't have the patience or compassion to be one. Needless to say there were no fond memories of him after he left – only relief.

Another event of significance was my confirmation upon reaching the age of twelve. On the morning of this important occasion, I remember kneeling under the kitchen table to polish my brother Padraic's shoes as he ate his breakfast. He had been very late getting up, and while he was eating I noticed his shoes were in need of a good clean. I didn't want him going to my confirmation with unpolished shoes, so I took an extreme measure and, despite being dressed for the event myself, decided to kneel under the table and polish his shoes for him.

My mother showed excellent taste in choosing my confirmation outfit, which was quite unusual but stylish. Most likely, it was bought in Gurteen, at either Jim Grady's or Seamus McGovern's, the two local draper shops. My wardrobe of that era was mainly made up of their clothing. The outfit consisted of a blue cardigan, pink shirt and tie, with a grey pinstripe trousers and black shoes.

The fear of God was put into me about getting confirmed. Clichés and innuendoes were rife that the bishop slapped everyone across the face during the ceremony. I foolishly believed this to be true, and I was very nervously expecting and dreading a slap across the face as I waited in line at the altar rails for his eminence to come my way. But there was no hard slap, merely a gentle stroke to the face as he asked what name I had chosen before giving me the blessing. I chose 'Martin' as my confirmation name due to the influence of a magazine and the devotion to St Martin that surrounded me at the time.

At this time Ireland had begun to pay special devotion to St Martin

De Porres, who is the patron saint of social justice, and I chose the name 'Martin' for my confirmation partly after him. He was born in Peru in 1579 and canonised a saint in 1962. He became particularly well known to me during my youth owing to the monthly Irish publication of *St Martin's Magazine*. The company in Dublin who published the magazine were very generous and supplied free religious goods to people who sold magazines on their behalf. I took out subscriptions for six magazines a month and sold them on to neighbours, including Nora and Marie in Brackloon. In return I was rewarded with rosary beads, prayer books and an assortment of medals for my efforts. I also liked *St Martin's Magazine* for another reason, it had a children's section with a monthly story about a dog named Fella, who was an office dog. The story usually entailed some escapade with Fella and his good friends. Fella lived with Jock Bruce Spider and Freddy Fly. Their other friends and acquaintances included Mr Frankie Fairy, Hetty Hen and her nine daughters and her son Christie Cock, Rosie Rat, Dickie and Denise Donkey, Annie Ass, Maureen Rabbit as well as Henrietta Horse and her four nice sons. It wasn't unlike George Orwell's *Animal Farm* in the sense that Fella and his friends enjoyed adventures, dramas and accidents and you read about them as if they were actually real animals living in a world where they resembled human characters. I always loved this story and looked forward to it every month.

Through no fault or choice of my own, I acquired very few male friends when I was younger, mainly because I was the only boy in my class. Furthermore, there were few boys in the higher or lower classes either, leaving me with little option but to get along with the girls. My cousin Veronica was seven months older than me, and she lived in a village close to my home. Her mother, my aunt, grew up in the same house as me, so we therefore had a close connection. Veronica and I went to the same primary school, and when we entered the senior classes, we shared the same desk. I don't know whether this happened by chance or because we were relatives, but I presume it was for the latter reason. Veronica in many ways was the sister I never had, and we visited each other fortnightly on alternate Sundays. I used to cycle over to her house, which was a two-mile journey or so, whilst Veronica's father or one of her brothers would drive her around to my home for the afternoon. These visits to her house were always pleasant occasions, as I loved Aunt Tess's hospitality.

There was one occasion when I feared this hospitality would be withdrawn after Veronica had an accident for which I was blamed. It was the autumn of our final year at primary school, and Veronica tripped on her shoelace, causing her to fall whilst she was running down the school driveway towards the bus. It was thought that she had only hurt herself slightly, but it later transpired that she had, in fact, broken her wrist. However, Veronica in some way or other felt the need to tell her mother that she had been playing at lunchtime and that I had either pushed or tripped her resulting in her falling. She thought that by implicating me, her mother wouldn't be angry with her for her giddiness. Charming. Thank you, Veronica! Perhaps, this was my comeuppance for all the times I had pushed her off the seat of the desk we shared. Now I could no longer do that – with her wrist in plaster – and I had to grin and bear being the 'culprit' for her accident.

Mrs Lynch became our head teacher for my final two years at St Joseph's, and I had serious reservations and fears about what she would be like before she arrived because she was a relative of the horrible headmaster who had just retired. But she soon proved to be quite different to him. It would have been impossible to compare them after I got used to her style and personality. In fact, if anything, I remember her with great fondness. Mrs Lynch cycled to school daily, and teaching at St Joseph's was to be her last post before retirement.

There were just four in my class – Mary Teresa, Martina, my cousin Veronica and myself. We got plenty of homework to do under Mrs Lynch's regime, and she was also eager to teach us catechism. However, my friends and I didn't always learn the catechism as she intended. She invariably gave us four questions and answers, and would ask us to learn the answers to these by heart. But we soon developed a trick where we each only learned one answer apiece. We observed that she always asked the pupil standing on her left the first question and then continued through the line to the end pupil on her right, and she never veered away from this system. We therefore came up with a cunning plan to ease the burden of having to learn all of the answers. Every day we would choose a question each to answer, and then the next day we would carefully place ourselves in the prearranged order we had agreed in advance. We had no contingency plan though and relied on the good luck that she didn't change tactics and start asking questions in a different direction.

I have never said as many prayers as I did in those days, and in many ways it was like serving an apprenticeship. Prayers were said four times daily with the first round taking place at 9 a.m. before classes began. There were more prayers at lunchtime and again at the close of the day before we went home. But the main prayers were said at ten to eleven each morning, and these often went on for at least twenty minutes. I doubt if there is any saint in the Catholic religion that I haven't prayed to or at least heard their life story. Take for instance St Bridget, whose feast day falls on February 1st. Mrs Lynch urged us to pay special devotion to her and delighted in telling us that she was born the daughter of an Irish chieftain in the fourth century. St Bridget became a nun because she had a special desire to help the poor, and one day on visiting a dying pagan chieftain, she sat on a small stool by his bedside and prayed to God to forgive him for his sins. St Bridget regretted that the dying man was an unbeliever and wondered how she could bring him closer to God in his final moments. It was then that a thought entered her mind as she gazed at the rushes strewn to cover the floor. She decided to weave him a cross from them so a rush cross would represent the significance of the Christian faith. After she had woven the cross, she placed it on the dying chieftain's bed. It was after this that the woven rush cross became forever synonymous with St Bridget.

One February Mrs Lynch came up with the idea that each of us should make a replica of St Bridget's cross to commemorate her anniversary, and we were asked to bring rush cuttings into school for this all-important task. This request wasn't difficult to fulfil because the west of Ireland isn't short of rushes; they grow in abundance in its damp fields. St Bridget's cross looks simple in design, and it was easy to be lured into thinking the task would be straightforward and quick to accomplish. Let me tell you, it was a struggle from the very start. I tried and tried to weave the rushes like Mrs Lynch had shown us, but I couldn't grasp the technique she seemed to have of getting it to gather into shape. Hand weaving is a little like knitting without needles, and I'm afraid my fingers weren't obliging enough to create a credible cross. Only one girl out of the senior classes seemed to create something that looked like St Bridget's design. The rest of my school friends, myself included, only managed to create designs that looked distinctly defective at best! I think even St Bridget would have been amused at our feeble efforts to recreate her masterpiece.

As I have already said, saying prayers during the course of my Irish Catholic childhood had become second nature. But at times this was monotonous and my attention often drifted away to a collage of drawings hung on the wall close to my desk which captured my imagination. A local nun had given the drawings to Mrs Lynch as a gift, depicting the story of a well-known Irish poem, *The Old Woman of the Roads* by Padraic Colum. Each of the poem's six verses had a drawing illustrating the story of the dream of a lonely itinerant woman. The drawings followed the story of the old woman's yearning for the security of living in a house of her own, of owning prized possessions and being able to go to sleep at night feeling the warmth and contentment of a turf fire. Here are the words of the poem:

> O, to have a little house!
> To own the hearth and stool and all!
> The heaped up sods against the fire,
> The pile of turf against the wall!
>
> To have a clock with weights and chains
> And pendulum swinging up and down!

A dresser filled with shining Delph,
Speckled and white and blue and brown!

I could be busy all the day
Clearing and sweeping hearth and floor,
And fixing on their shelf again
My white and blue and speckled store!

I could be quiet there at night
Beside the fire and by myself,
Sure of a bed and loth to leave
The ticking clock and the shining Delph!

Och! But I'm weary of mist and dark,
And roads where there's never a house or bush,
And tired I am of bog and road,
And the crying wind and the lonesome hush!

And I am praying to God on high,
And I am praying to Him night and day,
For a little house – a house of my own –
Out of the wind's and the rain's way.

I can't say that I was conscientious at doing homework for Mrs Lynch and sometimes put off doing any until the very last minute. More often than not, I could be found doing it in a panic at breakfast time. This often involved learning poems by rote in both English and in Gaelic. My friends and I considered this a boring task at the best of times but doubly so for poems which had to be learned in Gaelic. I never understood a word of what I was saying, and it was a constant guessing game as to whether or not one was pronouncing the words in the correct way. It was like creating a language that didn't exist with me inventing my own pronunciations of words, which were neither English nor Gaelic.

Learning English poems off by heart was moderately better. I recall learning *Hiawatha's Childhood* by Henry Longfellow, which had innocence about it, but at the same time contained a haunting and lonely presence. The first two verses of the poem went:

Then the little Hiawatha
Learned of every bird its language,
Learned their names and all their secrets,
How they built their nests in Summer,
Where they hid themselves in Winter,
Talked with them whene'er he met them,
Called them 'Hiawatha's Chickens'.

Of all the beasts he learned the language,
Learned their names and all their secrets,
How the beavers built their lodges,
Where the squirrels hid their acorns,
How the reindeer ran so swiftly,
Why the rabbit was so timid,
Talked with them whene'er he met them,
Called them 'Hiawatha's Brothers'.

One day Mrs Lynch was not impressed with a piece of homework I handed in for correction. The English exercise entailed listing the various outfits and uniforms worn by people in different professions. It was easy to write 'suit and tie' for a bank manager and 'overalls' for a mechanic, but when it came to teachers I got a little unstuck so I listed 'ordinary clothes' to describe what I felt teachers wore. Mrs Lynch got very upset by this statement and gave me an abrupt reprimand. I recall her snobbery with amusement when she rebuked me in an accusatory tone for having the audacity to imply that teachers wore casual clothing. She informed me the correct answer for teachers should have been 'a variety of clothes' and not 'ordinary clothes'.

Whilst I did have moments when I doodled and daydreamt, there were also times when I could be found in deep concentration. I discovered a concerted effort I had made on a piece of my homework when I stumbled across one of my old copybooks when researching this book. Whilst I was flicking through the pages, I came across a piece of geography homework which intrigued me. On one of the pages read this statement:

> No object really contains colour. A leaf might appear green to us but, in fact, what makes it green is only a reflection of white light. The white light itself is not white at all but a composition of seven colours …

My hunch is I must have copied this quotation from some textbook or other. I don't know whether the theory on light reflection is correct or not, but I assume it is. But this is irrelevant in any case because the quotation reveals a sense of mystery and ambiguity, and therefore its philosophy can be interpreted in ways other than just geographical matters. For me it is realising that behind every human character lies a multitude of different facets in the sense that we reveal ourselves to various people in different ways.

What is also interesting in the quotation is the use of the number seven. Note how there is a composition of seven colours in white light – not six or five. I don't know how many parts there can be to any individual, but I would reason that, to take an arbitrary number such as seven, leaves many facets to discover and get to know. I appreciate that these are philosophical thoughts, but I could not possibly have imagined when I wrote the piece over thirty years ago that I would return to it all these years later and dissect its meaning!

There were two rather amusing incidents at primary school that stick out in my mind. The first memorable occasion was when some stray cattle belonging to a neighbouring farmer broke into the school grounds. This wasn't the first time they had paid an impromptu visit, and I was promptly sent by Mrs Lynch to reprimand John, the owner of the cattle, whose house was next door to the school. She knew that the cattle belonged to him and was none too pleased about their trespassing. I was asked to inform him that his cattle had broken into the school grounds and to instantly remove them – and for him to mend his fence too! I went along with another lad, but he was younger than me so I had to act as spokesperson. I hated having to do this and wished that Mrs Lynch had done this unpleasant task herself.

John was out on the road talking to another man as we approached. I quickly blurted out what Mrs Lynch has sent me to say, bluntly relaying the message that she wanted him to mend the broken fence as a matter of urgency. John just stood there and didn't utter a word in his defence; he only nodded his head to acknowledge what I had said. I gave a sigh of relief after delivering the message, as I had feared that he might get angry with me. I need not have been afraid, however, because John had a quiet and gentle nature. I don't think he was too perturbed about Mrs Lynch's complaint and probably just ignored it because his cattle paid several more visits after this. Thankfully, I wasn't asked to go and visit him again with another rebuke.

The second incident involved my own perceptions of my astuteness. At the time I thought I was really clever and that I had a unique gift for being able to think fast in tricky situations. Mary, the bus driver, had informed Mrs Lynch that she was expecting a school transport inspector to pay her a visit sometime and that she feared she would get caught for only doing one school run instead of two. Admittedly, there were times when room on the bus felt a little tight, especially when ten or fifteen of us were on board, but this never bothered us in the least. The nature of the proposed visit meant that we didn't know when the inspector would show up, so Mrs Lynch assigned me the task each afternoon when Mary arrived at the school gates of going to ask her if she was going to do one or two school runs.

One day, I was halfway down the footpath to the bus when I suddenly noticed the school inspector talking to Mary. I gasped in horror and asked myself, 'What am I going to do?' Then suddenly I came up with an incredibly clever idea and started picking up litter on the school grounds. This gave me an excuse for being out of the building alone and prevented me from approaching Mary, which would, undoubtedly, have proved disastrous had I gone and asked her, in the presence of the inspector, how many school runs she was about to do. Returning to the classroom I told everyone what my solution had been, but instead of being complimented for my astuteness, I was surprised by the rebuke from Mrs Lynch: 'I wish you were as clever in class as you are at other things.' Instead of receiving some praise I was left crestfallen that I hadn't received recognition for my quick thinking.

During my latter years at St Joseph's I learned how to dance, or at least I tried my best to become a dancer. When I was in fifth class two dancing teachers came to our school for an hour's tuition every week, and they taught us various dances, but these were mostly jigs and reels. It was compulsory for everyone to join in the lessons, and whilst I was nervous and shy to begin with, I gradually increased my confidence and began to look forward to the weekly sessions. I think I began to take too much of an interest in my dancing, becoming rather obsessed with it, and I even dreamt of becoming a professional dancer. Of course, the best part of all was the practice during the week before the next lesson. This was mainly carried out at home in private as opposed to at school with my friends. When I say in private, I mean it was in the privacy of my own home but in close proximity to my family. Maybe this was the first time I shocked my family with my antics, as I can still remember the disbelief on the faces of my brothers when they watched me practising. I practised everywhere, in the kitchen, bathroom, bedrooms, outside on the back walk, and even in the sitting room where one or more of my brothers would be watching television. In my endless dedication to getting the steps of the jigs mastered, I managed to get on everyone's nerves. Shoes and newspapers often got thrown at me when I obstructed their view, but I carried on because I was determined to become a professional dancer and nobody was going to stop me.

At twelve I was very tall for my age, and people would tell me I had done my growing all at once. This was an Irish way of referring to young people who were taller than normal and who were considered lanky. I'm not sure what my height actually was, but I'm sure I wasn't far off five feet before I reached twelve. My height was particularly noticeable because I was quite thin as well as being tall. So this lanky boy nearly drove his parents and brothers to distraction with leaping about the place – all in the name of dance practice! My endurance paid off though because in the final weeks of primary school I won first prize in the male dancing competition. Such was my delight at winning that I had not given a second thought to the fact that others might have been surprised about it. My ego had taken it for granted that I would win, but after winning I was greeted with derision by others in my class instead of praise. They thought I had cheated and were genuinely surprised I had won since they considered me to be an awful dancer. It never occurred to me that I had won for my efforts as opposed to having genuine talent. After that, reality set in and my dreams of a dancing career were left behind, to the obvious relief of my family!

I always had a slightly sensitive side to my character, and I remember crying at the beginning of the summer holidays in 1974 after completing fifth class. For some unapparent reason I was overwhelmed with sadness that the class above me had finished their primary education. I reasoned that from thereon they would go their separate ways to secondary school, where they would make new friends so they would no longer be close with each other. I realised that whatever bond they had would be broken and that things would never be the same. Part of this was the realisation that I too would experience a similar fate, leaving the local school behind me in a year's time, and how daunting this would be.

My final year at primary school was uneventful in the main except that during the winter of 1974 we were given some time off school when President Erskin Childers, only the second Protestant to serve in this office in the Irish Republic, died. The day was to coincide with his state funeral, which was also a national day of mourning. I saw a picture of his body in one of the newspapers whilst he was lying in state, and the images triggered off the usual pattern of erratic sleeplessness and fear of the dark, even though, on this occasion, I had only seen a picture of the dead body. Similar occurrences, which had started at Jimmy Seamus's funeral, happened every time I saw dead bodies of neighbours.

Death is always daunting for young people, perhaps because it is not fully understood and because fear is an inevitable part of it. I must have seen at least twenty dead people whilst I was growing up, and each time the nights which followed were full of fear of the darkness. We had snow at the time of the president's funeral and I remember enjoying the time off school but dreading nightfall, for I knew what fear the darkness would bring. I loved daytime and would busy myself with my dog Captain or helping my father check his cattle. And then night would come. It was cosy being inside watching TV in front of a warm turf fire in the early part of the evening – but this was interrupted by the call for bedtime and the dreaded darkness. I had a picture card of St Martin de Porres sellotaped to the headboard of my bed in the hope of getting help in the situation. But alas it didn't work. Only daylight brought reassurance that something terrifying wouldn't poke its ugly head out from behind the curtains or from under the bed during the night.

My time at primary school was rapidly drawing to an end, and I discussed with my mother the possibility of buying Mary a present to thank her for all her fun and patience over the years of driving my friends and me to school. I was really happy with my mother's decision to buy her some perfume. Unfortunately, this was only decided on the evening before my last day at school. This left little time for the actual purchase. It was agreed that my mother would go to Gurteen to buy it and would then leave it on the top right-hand pier of the front wall for me to give to Mary when she dropped me off from school. My mother knew that I was due to get a half day, and would be home at 12.30 p.m. Sadly, things did not go according to plan. My mother's trip to Gurteen encountered an unexpected delay and hence she was not back in time to leave the present out for Mary. I was really excited as the bus drew nearer to our house, as I was expecting to see the parcel on the wall. I can still recall my disappointment on discovering its absence. In a crestfallen mood I mumbled a quiet goodbye to Mary. She never received her present, and I was never able to say a proper thank you to her. With hindsight, I could have asked my mother to deliver the perfume to her home or to post it, but for some reason or other neither of these options took place. My primary school days were over. The future beckoned as I prepared to enter the daunting world of secondary school and adolescence.

My Christening photograph with my parents and brothers.

The Henry brothers in ascending order –
Declan, Padraic, Kevin and John.

The Henry brothers in descending order –
John, Kevin, Padraic and Declan.

My first school photo. Cute, eh?

Padraic riding on Kitty, with our
Irish wolfhound Swift sniffing in the background.

Who is this angelic-looking little boy? It's me!
First Holy Communion, St. Joseph's Church, Rooskey, 1970.

*Our family home in Derrykinlough: the perfect childhood home.
My grandfather, Thomas Henry, built it in 1941.
His daughters, Bea and Mary (my aunts) had emigrated to
America, and helped pay for it by sending him some money.
The house was my grandfather's pride and joy and was
considered to be the nicest-looking house in the locality.*

Here I am visiting my father while he was working on the farm. I often went out looking for him after I got home from school. I always liked to see what he was doing and to tell him about my day. Father was never idle and was always found busily working on the land.

My parents and I after Mass one Sunday in 1972.
Notice Captain's head at the bottom of the photo!

I look in a sombre mood in this one for some reason.
But look at those beautiful flowers.

Me on my bicycle – smiling!

Padraic on his motorcycle – registration number JE1 645.

Mother and Padraic standing on the front lawn.

All happy smiles for the camera –
Padraic, me, John and my mother.

Confirmation day – May 1973

*My mother and I taken on my confirmation
day in the sitting room at home.*

My cousin Veronica and yours truly

Captain looking every bit the gorgeous dog he was.
I cried so much after he died.

Kevin and I. Check out his flamboyant shirt and tie!
This was the fashion of the seventies.

Mother and I after raiding my father's plum tree, 1974.

This is my mother's childhood home in Brackloon where Marie later lived.

Marie in the front garden at Brackloon.

Mother and Kevin taken on the road in Brackloon.
My mother retained great affection for Brackloon, where
she had spent her childhood years. My family and I
visited the village frequently and we too held it in high esteem.
There was something about the place that had great warmth.

4

Defining Moments of Christmas

My parents always put great effort and time into preparing for Christmas each year, and they were very special times in my home in Derrykinlough. When the season was near, we put up big and gaudy decorations, and we loved them. Nothing compared to the excitement of seeing our house transformed with Christmas cheer. The sitting room always received special treatment. Its timber ceiling easily accepted our drawing pins so we went particularly overboard with criss-crossing streamers with balloons added to each corner.

Nature made its contribution with the holly, which we raided from a neighbour's tree, a bicycle journey away. We cut it into small branches and placed it over pictures and high-rise furniture. We did not care whether they had berries or not. Berries were generally rare except for the occasional year when a full bloom would surprise us all.

One Christmas in the early seventies artificial trees were on display for purchase in Jim Grady's shop in Gurteen. We were all amazed at how real they looked, so my mother decided to buy one during one of her trips to the village. There was great excitement in our house when she arrived home with the parcel, and when it was unwrapped we thought it was the nicest tree we had ever seen. It was tall, broad and very convincing in its realism. At that time, it was unthinkable that anyone would assume it was anything but real, especially after we decorated it with tinsel and an assortment of differently shaped and coloured baubles.

Christmas heralded more frequent visits by the postman, who came daily with cards. We would line them up on the mantelpiece, and then the overflow would go on a specially constructed line of thread across one of the walls. We always counted how many we received to see if they outnumbered those of the preceding year. They usually did, but some years when the count seemed low we cheated a little by adding a

53

few of the cards stored away with the Christmas decorations from previous years. It was tempting to delude people into thinking we had
received more cards than we actually did, and I think it was my
brother Kevin who started this trend, but I soon caught on to the idea
too. However, one year we were over the moon when the real number
amounted to over thirty cards. We thought our popularity was at an
all-time high.

Something else stands out in my memory of earlier Christmases:
the big market fairs in Tubbercurry. This annual event on December
8th attracted large crowds since it was the place to go for Christmas
gifts and, not least, to buy a turkey. Buying a turkey was no easy task,
and my father would cast an experienced eye over all the birds until he
spotted one he judged to be healthy and well fed. In the meantime
many jokes were exchanged and plenty of bartering took place. It
wasn't uncommon to hear a reply to a trader asking for too high a
price like, 'Aarrah … What are you talking about? I wouldn't give the
butt of a fag for that,' when negotiations took a turn for the worse.

Eventually, a live turkey would be purchased and taken home,
where its health and happiness would continue to be watched over
until a few days before Christmas. Then it would be slaughtered,
plucked and cleaned in time for dinner on the day itself.

Christmas time also meant an extended story about Fella, the office
dog, in the December edition of *St Martin's Magazine*. I would eagerly
await and read the story longing to see what the twist would be at the
end. Here is one of the stories:

> Hello, Boys and Girls,
>
> Oh, what an awful fright we got as Jock Bruce Spider put his hand
> in his pocket and took out the letters that were to be posted two weeks
> ago telling Santa what we wanted. Freddy Fly sarcastically said that if
> we woke up on Christmas morning and found nothing, Jock would be
> the first to call Santa names and say how mean he was.
>
> Jock and I rushed downstairs to listen to what Freddy Fly and Mr
> Fairy would say and to see if anything could be done for us. Freddy
> handed the letter to the Fairy and said: 'That stupid Spider is going to
> ruin our Christmas'. Jock said to me: 'Fella! I think Freddy Fly might

sometimes be right, I think I am stupid.' All I did was to give a big growl and make a bite at him. I said that besides being stupid he was unreliable, and I made another bite at him.

All this time the Fairy kept looking at the letters and turning them over in his hand, saying: 'Mr Fly, you are asking an awful lot. Do you know you are asking me to break the first law of Toyland, which is that all letters must be posted so that they will be received at least three days before Christmas? You beg me to bring your letter by hand just hours before Santa leaves! Oh! Mr Fly, you are asking a lot, but put on the kettle and we will have a chat and see if anything can be done'.

Jock looked at me and said: 'Fella, Santa will be leaving in a few hours and all that Fairy wants to do is sit there drinking tea. I know we are going to have a very sad and lonely Christmas.' All I did was to give another growl and make another bite at him reminding him once again that it was all his fault. Boys and Girls, it was just awful listening to Mr Fairy talking about football, and where he was when he was small, and all the time drinking cup after cup of tea but still there was no sign of him going. From where we were hiding we could see our three letters sticking out of his pocket and once again Jock said: 'I hope he does not forget to deliver them'.

At last Freddy Fly said: 'Mr Fairy, I hope you remember the letters you have in your pocket, for in a few hours Santa will be leaving'. With that the Fairy jumped up and said: 'I nearly forgot about the letters! Please let me out. Freddy Fly why didn't you remind me? I'm late already and by the look of things I can't see myself being in time for Santa before he leaves. Perhaps he will not even take delivery of them.' With that he finished his tenth cup of tea and dashed for the door shouting: 'Happy Christmas'.

When Mr Fairy left, Jock Bruce Spider and I rushed over to Freddy Fly who said: 'Men! Things are looking bad. I cannot see that Fairy getting those letters to Toyland in time. If he is late it should be a lesson to every little boy and girl all over the world to post their letters in time and not expect Santa to bring the toys if he doesn't get the letters'. Then Freddy said that the best thing for us to do was to go to bed and hope that, maybe, Mr Fairy would be back in time and we would not have to go back to play with our last year's toys.

Jock and I went to bed and I felt sorry for poor Jock as he wept and said: 'It is all my fault! As Freddy said I'm stupid, I'm stupid!' Well,

Boys and Girls, I do remember getting into my basket, but I don't remember going asleep for all of a sudden I woke and there was Jock Bruce Spider dressed up like an Indian and screaming: 'Fella, Fella, Santa came after all! A Happy Christmas Freddy Fly and Fella'.

Oh, Boys and Girls, I jumped out of my box and there stood a lovely, gleaming three-wheel tricycle with the words 'For a good Dog. Happy Christmas from Santa'. Well, I could hardly believe my eyes to see such a lovely present. So Mr Fairy got back in time to Santa in Toyland and we all had a Happy Christmas with all our lovely presents. We hope you have the same. Until next month, three barks and a wag of my tail! Woof! Woof! Woof! Fella.

The idea of Santa Claus was very much alive in my house. I recall waking before dawn on Christmas morning and looking at the gap at the bottom of my bedroom door to see if I could see a light on in the sitting room. If I did, I knew my mother was up, and without further thought I would leap out of bed and race to the sitting room to see if Santa had indeed come. And there on the table would be a wrapped brown parcel waiting for me. The thrill and excitement of getting the string off added to the agonising suspense of the moment. Many coveted gifts would be revealed: train sets, colouring books, pens and plasticine – Christmas had well and truly arrived.

What never seemed to arrive though was snow. I recall Christmas Eve as having a distinctive peacefulness about it. Snow certainly wouldn't have been out of place then, and I remember often longing for a white Christmas. I think that Christmas cards picturing a pristine all-white world fostered the anticipation of snow, and maybe it was just as well we kept the nicer cards for redisplay because no snow made its appearance in the Christmases of my youth. The weather unfortunately always remained mild.

My mother switched on all the lights in our house on Christmas Eve, and a candle was placed on the kitchen windowsill. This was symbolic to show that our Lady and St Joseph were welcome in our house. This touching simplicity reminded us of the Christmas story, and that it was the beginning of a joyous time to be cherished and enjoyed.

Christmas Day was usually very relaxing in our house. After Mass, my brothers and I helped our father with the necessary farm jobs, but we did them as quickly as possible. The essential turf for mother's fire was brought in while she had the very serious task of cooking the Christmas dinner. 'Keep that fire well stoked,' was a remark often to be heard coming from her lips. The table was always meticulously laid with mother's best table linen and crockery.

Films on television were limited, but anything with dinosaurs or something that would frighten or thrill would add another few hours' enjoyment to an already perfect day. A few neighbours or my god-father, would come to visit in the latter part of the evening, with my parents usually doing the chatting and entertaining.

St Stephen's Day was special too. Ireland has a long tradition involving something called 'wren-boys'. This focuses around the wren – a little brown bird similar in appearance and size to a robin but without a red breast. Stories about the wren come from mythology dating back to the Middle Ages. The Irish word for wren is *dreán* or *draoi éan*, which translates as 'druid bird', and according to ancient folklore the wren is quite a mischievous little bird. Allegedly, when the Irish forces were about to catch Cromwell's troops by surprise, a wren perched on one of the soldier's drums and made a loud noise. This noise woke the rival troops in time to fight the Irish soldiers, resulting in many casualties. Another tale blames the wren for betraying St Stephen, who was the first Christian martyr. Apparently, St Stephen was hiding from his attackers, but a nearby wren flapped its wings, alerting the pursuers to his hiding place. Evidently, because of these misdemeanours a folklore king dictated that all wrens should be hunted down and killed. Thankfully, a less harsh interpretation of this command was in place several centuries on and all that was required was to sing or play a musical instrument on December 26th. Perhaps this was punishment enough for the wrens, having to listen to croaky voices and musical malfunctions of many youths, when otherwise they could be perched peacefully on trees. A financial reward was usually given at the end of each wren performance. This is a little verse which explains the process a little more:

The wren, the wren,
the king of all birds
On Stephen's Day
was caught in the furze
Up with the kettle
down with the pan
Give us a penny
to bury the wren.
If you haven't a penny
a ha'penny will do
If you haven't a ha'penny
God Bless You.

I personally went out on the 'wren' for four years in a row; the first two with an older friend, and after he had outgrown the experience a different friend accompanied me for another two years. I can't remember what I sang with the first friend, it could well have been a rendition of either *Silent Night* or *Rudolph the Red Nosed Reindeer*. However, during the final two years my act became more refined in the sense that I chose a song by Brendan Shine, an Irish country and western singer, entitled *Where the Three Counties Meet*.

Throughout my wren career, I always cycled from house to house with my partner. We travelled around for at least eight hours, covering a dozen or so of the local rural villages with our act. Our trips took us through muddy boreens and over fences; we were often attacked by dogs, and knocked on dozens of doors before singing our song. But there was a tremendous excitement about travelling around and singing in public. Some people were kind enough to give us chocolates and biscuits as well as money. I left the task of 'cashier' to my partners. They collected the money throughout the day and at the end we went to one of our houses and split our earnings equally.

I will always remember Brendan Shine's song with its jovial lyrics:

Oh how lovely to be on the shores of Lough Ree
On a beautiful mid summer's morning
Looking over the lake where the waters do break
By the hills in the County Roscommon

I left my home, in the town of Athlone
On the way to the Three Jolly Pigeons
It was near Glasson town, on the road I sat down
And looked over the beautiful Shannon

Lough Ree, oh Lough Ree, where the three counties meet
Longford, Westmeath and Roscommon
As I stroll round her banks, by the heather and peat
They're the memories I've never forgotten

Oh sad was the day, that I went away
To work among timbers and concrete
For now as a man, I must follow life's plan
I forsook the dear place of my homeland

If God grants me grace, I'll return to the place
When the sunset of life has come o'er me
Once again on these shores, like a bird my heart soars
As I gaze on the beauty around me.

I would arrive home at the end of the day, just before dusk, exhausted and dirty, although I was richer than at the beginning of it. My mother would have something lovely and warm ready for me to eat, and I would go to bed afterwards feeling very happy. The exuberance of innocence and youth was in full flow. Christmas time was simply brilliant!

5

Why Priest?

I remember my father telling a story about a priest who was once in our parish when he was a young man. The parish priest had come to the home of one of our neighbours in Derrykinlough to say Mass. It was customary in those days for neighbours in each village to take it in turns to have Mass in their homes, and they would invite other neighbours and friends to attend. However, on this occasion the priest got a shock when he arrived and discovered that adequate preparation hadn't been put into arranging the event – there were no candlesticks on the makeshift altar. The priest quickly remonstrated with the man of the house in front of his family and neighbours for having no candlesticks on the altar. There was of course a simple explanation for this. The poor man didn't own any candlesticks and had forgotten to borrow them from somewhere else. This happened during the 1940s when priests were never criticised in Irish life. The neighbour felt mortified at the priest's anger and felt compelled to go immediately and borrow some candlesticks from a neighbouring house, holding up the service in the meantime. At the time people were deeply embarrassed that the priest had been put in such a difficult situation. Criticism was firmly pointed towards the man, whom they believed should have been thoroughly ashamed of himself for allowing such a situation to occur.

My parents were from a generation of people who had total respect for the Catholic Church and its clergy, and they were as accustomed to this as they were to the blood in their veins. The clergy of the land dispensed God's law and to challenge this authority was unthinkable. There wasn't the slightest hint that sexual atrocities with children were being freely perpetrated in their midst. However, the seventies saw attitudes beginning to shift, with people realising that some of the men and women in religious life were not very nice people. My father was now comfortable enough to say how wrong the priest had been to publicly insult and shame his neighbour. The pathway was being paved, without knowing, for the decades to follow when people would freely challenge the clerical misuse of power that culminated in the sexual abuse scandals.

Priests in our parish invariably held the title of 'Canon'. Then there were the curates, who tended to be younger priests and who came and went after an average stay of a year. Occasionally though, an older curate was promoted to the position of Canon. As a family, we attended church every Sunday without exception, and part of the preparation for attending Mass started at midnight on Saturday when fasting for Communion began. Thankfully, I never had to follow this ritual because by the time I had my First Communion at the age of seven, the Catholic Church had changed this arrangement and fasting only became compulsory an hour before the start of Mass.

Admittedly, there were times when my brothers and I breached even this amended fasting rule, often eating after the 9 a.m. deadline. We often thought ourselves to be cunning if our mother didn't notice us eating whilst she was busy getting dressed for Mass. But irrespective of whether she caught us or not, guilt would soon settle in after our arrival at church when the priest made reference to fasting and the importance of it in his sermon. In the priest's opinion, it was a sin to eat an hour before Mass time. Therefore, as a sin, this warranted a visit to the confessional. However, this rule too, like many before it in the Catholic Church, changed with time, and towards the end of my adolescence, fasting before Communion had become totally obsolete.

During my younger years, many people predicted that I would become a priest, and serving Mass in part fuelled this belief. The other reason was because I was the youngest son in my family, and in Irish society it was often customary for the youngest child, who was generally considered to bear less responsibility than the older siblings, to enter a religious life. However, my family, who saw another side of Declan, did not share this opinion. At home, I was the opposite of being quiet, shy and reserved. In fact, I loved having fun but was also capable of being petulant and opinionated.

Nevertheless, I remained very dutiful at serving Mass, as I really liked it and put great effort into getting the various tasks attached to it correct. The candles had to be lit, and the offertory water and wine had to be put out on a side table close to the altar. A primary task was the ringing of the bell when the priest consecrated the bread and wine. Fearing a feeble sound, I always gave the bell a rather hefty ring.

Helping with the service of Holy Communion was also part of my duties. In those days, parishioners could only take Communion on their tongues and never in their hands. My part was to help the priest by holding a bronze platter under the person's chin just in case the priest accidentally dropped the Communion or the recipient coughed and expelled it from their mouths. Neither of these scenarios ever happened, but that didn't stop me from speculating about the excitement and intrigue were something like this to occur. It was often boring just standing there watching people hang their tongues out.

There is an old Irish Communion hymn named *Cead Mile Failte Romhat a Iosa* that I really liked. It had a very simple meaning – its lyrics offering a thousand welcomes to Jesus, whom we were about to receive in Holy Communion, reminding us to give glory and praise to Him in return for the honour of Him coming into our lives. I imagine myself then, when not serving Mass, singing it in the church choir surrounded by girls whose delicate voices accompanied mine and all trying our utmost to sing together in a way which would conceal our individual voices. Here is the hymn in Irish:

> Cead mile failte romhat, a Iosa, a Iosa
> Cead mile failte romhat, a Iosa,
> Cead mile failte romhat a Shlanaitheoir,
> Cead mile, mile failte romhat, a Iosa, a Iosa.
>
> Glóir agus moladh duit, a Iosa, a Iosa,
> Glóir agus moladh duit, a Iosa,
> Glóir agus moladh duit, a Shlanaitheoir
> Glóir, moladh agus buiochas duit, a Iosa, a Iosa.

Translated into English the hymn reads as follows:

> A hundred thousand welcomes to you o Jesus, o Jesus
> A hundred thousand welcomes to you o Jesus
> A hundred thousand welcomes to you o Saviour
> A hundred thousand welcomes to you o Jesus, o Jesus.

> Glory and praise to you o Jesus, o Jesus
> Glory and praise to you o Jesus,
> Glory and praise to you o Saviour
> Glory, praise and thanks to you o Jesus, o Jesus.

Throughout my time at St Joseph's school I helped to serve Mass at funerals. It may seem selfish to say, but I loved it when there was a funeral because this meant a good chance of getting the morning off school to either serve Mass or sing in the choir. My classmates and I used to walk over from the school to the church, which was less than a mile away. Funeral Masses were classed as High Masses with three priests always presiding over the ceremony. During the early seventies there was no shortage of priests in the west of Ireland parishes. Each parish had at least two – which meant each priest, usually the curate, alternated between neighbouring parishes when called upon to assist at funeral Masses. At a funeral Mass, the clergy always wore black vestments, which gave added formality and reverence to the service. Local funerals were mainly of people who had lived and worked in the parish all their lives. They were of people who were bonded by a close sense of community and who had the respect and affinity of friends and neighbours they had known all throughout their lives. Members of the bereaved family rarely read from the testament or gave speeches eulogising the departed and there were no fresh flowers. There was no music either except a handful of schoolchildren singing hymns keeping the ceremony plain in nature. However, there was much beauty to be found in this simplicity.

As an altar boy, one of my duties was to light the incense holder by firstly lighting the charcoal in the thurible. The celebrant priest used to fan the incense smoke over the coffin as a symbol that God was ready to receive the soul of the departed into heaven. However, lighting the incense holder didn't always go exactly to plan. I often struggled with it because it seemed to have a mind of its own. The charcoal was either stubborn to light, or upon lighting would over smoke, resulting in the fumes filling the sacristy with a pungent mist. I recall my frequent panic as I battled to prevent the smoke from getting into the altar area of the church. Doors had to be quickly closed and windows opened as I attempted to fan the smoke away as quickly as possible. I feared the congregation would think a fire, which would burn down the entire church, had broken out in the sacristy. Thankfully, this never happened, and I was therefore saved from the embarrassment of having to flee the sacristy screaming 'Fire, Fire'.

I must confess to a certain fascination with altar wine, and I longed to know its taste. One day when I was alone in the sacristy I decided to carry out a little experiment. I risked opening the bottle in the cupboard where the priest's vestments were hung and took a very quick sip. It tasted delicious; similar to the sherry my mother had at home which was reserved for visitors. What sin had I committed? I can now imagine myself in James Joyce's brilliant description of hell from his book *A Portrait of an Artist as a Young Man*. I could have been a drunken altar boy who had achieved notoriety in his parish for an evil and wicked deed. Thankfully, however, my curiosity-fuelled misdemeanour didn't lead to any unfortunate result. I wasn't caught, and I have never divulged my secret to anyone – until now that is.

I can only recount my time as an altar boy with fond memories, and included in these memories are several priests, young, middle-aged and elderly, with varied personalities who passed through the parish over the years. But I have chosen to tell you about two priests in particular whom I consider as having great humility and character.

One of them, Canon Casey, was a quietly spoken man with a very gentle manner. He wore galoshes on rainy days, which I had never seen anyone wear before, and I was generally quite amused by their appearance. He also wore a long soutane and a hat.

After serving at funeral Masses and when the cortège had left on its journey to the cemetery, Canon Casey would give the altar boys a lift back to the school in his small blue Fiat car. He was usually in a hurry, as he had to go to the cemetery via a different route in order to meet the cortège when it arrived and to offer prayers at the graveside. This meant having to keep an eye on the clock. Sometimes after the funeral Mass ended people would come into the sacristy to speak to him, delaying him even further, and then he would have to change out of his vestments as well before leaving.

On one occasion, we were very late leaving the church, so Canon Casey put his foot on the accelerator and off we went at what appeared to be a breakneck speed. My friends in the back seat were laughing hilariously, which in turn, had me bursting into fits of laughter, which I had to desperately suppress as I was sitting next to the Canon in the passenger seat. Conversation was sparse in the car, which was not unusual since the Canon was quiet by nature, but on this occasion there was even less talk as we sped vigorously through Rooskey. The Canon seemed to forget his passengers completely, and none of us said anything to remind him to stop when we reached the school. We secretly hoped he would drive on to the cemetery without remembering to drop us off. It would have been lovely to have missed more lessons but suddenly he stamped on the brake after remembering his error, making everyone in the car, including himself, jerk forward. Remember this was in an era before wearing seatbelts was compulsory. Stopping so quickly produced more laughter from everyone. We considered the Canon to be more amusing by being himself than he could ever have imagined.

I recall another occasion when the Canon came to our school on one of his monthly visits. During these visits we would assemble around Mrs Lynch's table, where she would be seated with the Canon standing next to her. He would usually talk to us about some religious matter, but one day he told us a story of when he stayed in a hotel in Dublin, where the night before a guest had worshipped the devil. My young Catholic ears popped up to listen attentively to this story. I knew I was about to experience shivers of horror and feelings of curiosity like those I had felt after reading those ghost stories in the *Daily Mirror* that father had sent us from England. The Canon spoke slowly whilst telling the story and occasionally closed his eyes when emphasising a point. He didn't go into much detail about the background to the story and only stated that a trusted source had informed him that a well-known Satanist had stayed in the same hotel. The moment he entered his bedroom he sensed evil and was convinced that this was the room that the Satanist had used. The Canon was unable to sleep that night and passed the hours by continuously praying to counteract the evil in his surroundings. I remember standing, conjuring up an image of what the room looked like and wondering what it would have felt like to have stayed in a room by myself, not to mention sleeping in a bed alone in this chilling set of circumstances.

On another occasion the Canon discussed the issue of capital punishment and talked about how a murderer might repent his sin. I was able to conjure up a picture of a cruel and violent man in prison. The prisoner had been found guilty of the brutal murder of another man and had been jailed for life. I pictured him alone and destitute in his prison cell, but as the years passed the prisoner became guilt-ridden for murdering another human being and repented. He prayed to God for forgiveness and was instantly pardoned because of the honesty of his plea. The Canon and Mrs Lynch questioned what if the prisoner had been subjected to the death penalty and had been executed before having an opportunity to seek God's forgiveness? This rhetorical question was meant to illustrate how someone who feels remorseful can approach God and ask for forgiveness, but remorse for cruel actions can take time to set in and time is not available to someone sentenced to death.

Years later, I was saddened when the Canon announced to the congregation at Mass one Sunday that he felt his life was drawing to a close. In fact, he passed away just a few months later aged eighty-two. Nowadays, when I find myself in the churchyard where he is buried I always visit his grave, reflecting on his gentle character and the humility that this contained.

Father Burke, on the other hand, was much younger. He was in his early fifties and had a speech impediment which sometimes made it difficult to understand exactly what he was saying. However, he had warmth and an infectious laugh that endeared him to people enormously. Father Burke had a very down-to-earth approach, devoid of all airs or graces, and thus his popularity was even more enhanced. He would call at my home every month when it was his time to visit the sick and elderly in our neighbourhood, and my mother would always make tea. If her offer was slow in coming he would light-heartedly ask for it.

On one occasion when we were approaching Hallowe'en, my mother made Father Burke his usual mug of tea – he preferred a mug instead of a teacup and saucer. Hallowe'en meant it was a time for *bracks*. A *brack* is a fruit loaf that is always eaten with butter. It can be eaten at any time of the year, but what makes Hallowe'en special is that a ring is wrapped in paper and put in the dough. Apprehension and excitement lie in eating the *brack*, especially in a group setting when everyone is wondering who will get the ring in their piece. Folklore states that whoever gets the ring will be the next person to get married. This was obviously a myth intended for the benefit of children, and as a child it never dawned on me what would happen if the person who got the ring were indeed already married! On this occasion, my mother offered Father Burke a slice of *brack* with his tea. He quickly declined, 'Oh my God – what if I get the ring? – No thank you, ma'am.' I can't remember who actually got the ring on that occasion, but I do recall all of us laughing for a long time afterwards at Father Burke's swift refusal.

My job was to escort Father Burke to the various houses in neighbouring villages, and guide him to where the various elderly and sick people lived. On the way I used to give him some background information about their characters. Father Burke liked a little gossip, but it was rather harmless chitchat with me usually just informing him of recent visitors to the area or if someone had bought a new car.

Sadly, he died a few years later after leaving the parish. His death was premature as he was still only in his fifties, but his unassuming nature left behind kind memories which I have always remembered.

Is it real shamrock or clover? This question was often asked when people walked into Mass on St Patrick's Day. It was mainly shamrock which people actually wore, but every now and then an elderly man or woman – or occasionally not so elderly – would enter the church making the faux pas of displaying a big bunch of clover on the lapel of their jacket or coat, believing that it was in fact shamrock. Admittedly, baby clover could sometimes be mistaken for shamrock but is usually larger. I often helped my mother look for shamrock the day before St Patrick's Day, and more often than not, we could be found frantically searching the undergrowth of the ditch across from our house, or in the front lawn close to the flower-border edges. We usually found a few stems, which we would gather into small bunches and ration amongst us to pin on our lapels. I never really minded whether I wore shamrock or not and usually settled for wearing a green badge with a picture of St Patrick on it.

St Patrick's Day was always special in my youth, not least because it was a church holiday, which meant getting the day off school. We always attended Mass where we would sing with great pride and heartiness a hymn dedicated to our patron saint.

> Hail, glorious St Patrick, dear saint of our Isle,
> On us thy poor children bestow a sweet smile;
> And now thou art high in the mansions above,
> On Erin's green valleys look down in thy love.
>
> On Erin's green valleys, on Erin's green valleys,
> On Erin's green valleys look down in thy love.
>
> Hail, glorious St Patrick, thy words were once strong
> Against Satan's wiles and an infidel throng;
> Not less is thy might where in heaven thou art;
> O, come to our aid, in our battle take part.

Why Priest?

On Erin's green valleys, on Erin's green valleys,
On Erin's green valleys look down in thy love.

Street parades to commemorate the occasion were fairly rare in local towns during the seventies. There were parades in the larger towns but I never went to any of these, and I don't recall any of my friends or their families going either. Some of my friends cheated on St Patrick's Day because they believed it was acceptable to break Lenten pledges because it was considered such a special day. So sweets and chocolate were readily eaten with abstaining commencing again the next day until Easter Sunday. I never objected to this cheating and joined my friends in their indulgence without argument.

Our home in Derrykinlough was about fifty-five miles from Croagh Patrick – the holy mountain situated in County Mayo informally known in Ireland as the 'Reek'. This is where in the year 441 AD St Patrick is believed to have spent forty days and nights alone in the bitter cold at the top of the mountain, fasting and contemplating in prayer.

An annual pilgrimage on the last Sunday of July each year involved climbing three miles up to the top of the mountain and attending Mass. The climb was quite difficult and took over two hours, the last half a mile mainly consisted of scrambling over rocks and stones, making the ascent to the summit quite treacherous. A stick was essential for support, and my father always cut one especially for me. But the Order of Malta Ambulance Corps were always on standby with volunteers ready to administer first aid to anyone who fell or to take pilgrims with more serious injuries to hospital. On reaching the top, it was generally considered obligatory to attend confessions and Mass in the tiny chapel there. Several other rituals, however, had to be maintained during the climb, including doing a Station of the Cross at the halfway point.

When I was a very young child climbs rarely commenced in daylight and were mainly at night time. I remember my mother and brothers being collected by neighbours at around 10 p.m. as I was getting ready for bed. I envied them going on what seemed a mysterious voyage to me. My father always stayed at home to mind me; in fact, he only climbed the Reek once. He found it difficult he said and never felt the need to make a second pilgrimage. With having the 'young one', as I was referred to, at home to baby-sit, I provided him with the perfect excuse to stay behind.

I listened with fascination to the stories my mother and brothers brought back. They included tales of people climbing by flashlight and some without any light at all; itinerant women carrying young children on their backs, some in bare feet – others falling and getting cut. Stories of good humour and camaraderie, with strangers keeping an eye out for each other – everyone united in his or her faith, determined to serve God by undertaking the climb as an act of penance.

The summit of the Reek was always bitterly cold. Thick fog and mist as well as a sharp breeze greeted people as they walked around the church whilst saying a decade of the rosary. When I first climbed the Reek I expected the church to be similar in size and design to other Catholic churches, but I discovered it was very small and had no altar or pews inside. It was used for confessions and sections were partitioned off just for this purpose. Mass was celebrated every half an hour from 8 a.m. onwards in a little kiosk attached to one of the church gables, where people gathered in a large circle to participate. The church was built in the early 1900s, and what a remarkable achievement it was to build a church on top of a mountain three miles above ground level. Donkeys would have been used to carry every stone up there because in those days there was no other way.

Legend has it that to get to heaven pilgrims have to climb the Reek on three consecutive years to earn the privilege, so I duly climbed it three years in a row. It was during one of these climbs that I discovered 'the third station' when being accompanied by Beatrice, a family friend. Someone gave me a prayer leaflet at the bottom before we began the climb, and it was from this that I discovered an additional part of the pilgrimage once you reached the summit. It was optional, but Beatrice and I decided to do this extra act of penance consisting of climbing down the opposite side of the mountain for a mile or so. Few pilgrims did the third station because not many knew about it, whilst others decided not to take the risk. The task entailed finding the way through thick fog down to three separate boulders where one had to recite seven Hail Marys and seven Our Fathers around each clump. The next year, just before setting out for the climb, I can remember hearing my father say, 'God, ye'll end up in the sea if ye're not careful,' fearful that we would go off track in the heavy fog and get lost. Apart from being an arduous task, it was doubly hazardous, especially if there was an accident, as the Order of Malta didn't cover this isolated part of the mountain and therefore weren't on standby to assist in the event of us having an accident. It was indeed the 'survival of the fittest'.

I found the descent from Croagh Patrick to be delightful and easy, but not everyone would agree with me that this was the case. Many people considered it more difficult climbing down than going up, not just because it took longer but because of the danger of slipping on the rocks.

During the descent the majestic scenery of Clew Bay across in the distance made the physical challenge all the more worthwhile. The lake, hills and multitude of greenery made a delightful picture. The fog and mist had usually disappeared by the time you had got halfway down, making the views even more breathtaking. It was a relief to reach level ground once again because by that stage I usually felt physically exhausted, yet mentally refreshed. Stallholders at the bottom of the mountain sold religious memorabilia, and purchasing a medal or picture of St Patrick was a fitting end to the pilgrimage. It was then time to sit down and enjoy sandwiches and to be smugly satisfied that some of the people at the bottom of the mountain were just starting out on their climb. At this stage, after my own strenuous efforts, I believed that their task ahead was unenviable to say the least.

6

Saved by the Bell

I was very nervous when I started secondary school. A new chapter of my life was opening up, but I wasn't the least bit excited. To leave behind the comforts of my old surroundings and friends and go to a new environment filled me with apprehension and dread. There were three types of secondary school in Ireland in the 1970s. The first two were religiously managed: for example, convent schools run by nuns and then colleges run by priests or brothers. Technical (vocational) schools were the third choice, and young people were sent to these if they or their parents had aspirations for them to become carpenters, architects or toolmakers. Young people in schools like these were given tuition in practical subjects like woodwork, metalwork and technical drawing so they could go on afterwards to do apprenticeships in certain trades. All my brothers went to vocational schools, and thus it was no surprise that my parents chose this type of school for me. The vocational school in Tubbercurry was small with only about a hundred students, mainly boys, but it had a good reputation for successfully leading its school leavers into skilled careers. Apart from the practical and technical subjects the school offered a full curriculum that included English, Irish, Mathematics, History, Geography, Science, French, Civics (similar to Personal, Social and Health Education) and Religious Education. Cooking was off limits for boys with Domestic Science firmly a female subject on the curriculum. I would have loved to have learned how to cook but there was an ingrained mentality in school circles that cooking was only for girls. I had no alternative but to go along with this because if I didn't I'd have risked being called a 'cissy'.

Although there were one or two very intelligent students in my class, the rest, including myself, were generally of mixed academic ability. However, at least three of the boys in my year were illiterate, and it

72

seemed incredible that they had progressed from primary school to secondary school without the basic skills of being able to read or write. Whatever progress I made or ability I had in academic subjects, I simply was not gifted with practical skills. A cold sweat often ran down my back when it was time to enter the woodwork room or go into metalwork class. It was clear to me at the time that I would never be skilled in any of these subjects – not that I ever had any burning ambitions to be so.

My shortcomings were, for instance, well demonstrated in the subject of mechanical drawing. During these lessons my sketching of an elevation, end view and plan never matched up. In fact, they were usually way off the mark. I used to look around at my peers and wonder how they managed to make theirs match. My experiences in woodwork were no better. Any piece of timber I worked on ended up having wide gaps, and this really frustrated me. I hated chisels, planes and screwdrivers, which resulted in me invariably having my fingers covered in plasters. Metalwork was only marginally better, and except for my fear of electric drills and the lathe machine, I generally preferred it to the other technical subjects.

My journey to school began each morning with me cycling a mile from home to the end of the road, where I would catch the school bus to Tubbercurry. This seven-mile journey entailed many stops along the way to pick up other pupils. Travelling on the bus brought its own challenges too. There were many different personalities amongst the group, some nice, others horrid but harmless, but overall there was friendly camaraderie mixed in with squabbles, fistfights and name-calling.

The main form of heating in the vocational school were the coal stoves that Jimmy Johnston, the school caretaker, fuelled at regular intervals. Heat from the stoves went from one extreme to the other. It was unbearably hot in the morning as the coal kindled and freezing cold by late afternoon when the stoves ran low on fuel.

There wasn't any kind of school uniform, which meant students wore their own clothes to school. I was fortunate enough to have older brothers who had plenty of clothes to hand down or to lend me. There were of course advantages and disadvantages to this. I was tall and skinny, which meant the clothes were occasionally ill fitting in one way or another. Nevertheless, that aside, I am sure that during my six years of secondary school, I displayed a varied wardrobe mixed with some rather interesting fashion statements. This included different kinds of check and pinstripe as well as leather jackets, which were all the vogue at the time. But I can't help thinking that a school uniform would have been easier and indeed more suitable.

The vocational school was situated at the top of Piper Hill in Tubbercurry, alongside Church Street, which had a housing estate called Connolly Park on its left-hand side that was built in the 1930s. All this area was at that time regarded as the poorer end of the town. Perhaps one of the reasons for this was the assumed laziness associated with the men who lived there. The men were even believed to have boasted about their idleness in a rhyme which they composed, that went something like this:

> We are the men from Piper Hill
> We have never worked and
> We never will.
> We rob and steal* and
> We go to jail but
> Work we never will.

Every day I used to walk up and down this hill from the town square, where the school bus dropped and collected us. Some of the houses on the hill were in a bad state of repair and bordered on the threshold of poverty. Winter evenings saw the sky ablaze with smog; all the chimneys in close proximity to each other puffing smoke from the coal burning in the grates. Overall, the scene prompted a sense of unaesthetic greyness and loneliness.

---

* pronounced 'stale'

Tubbercurry was similar in size to Ballymote and contained a selection of shops, public houses, chemists, hardware shops and a few clothes shops. There were two factories on the outskirts of Tubbercurry, which generated business for the community. Right in the centre of the main street was Towey's pub and shop. There was a side room off the shop where tea, coffee and sandwiches were served, and women and children used this room as an alternative to the bar, which was mainly frequented by men. It was only a small room with no more than four tables in it, and it had Venetian blinds on the window looking out onto the street. I always sat by the window table because the blinds were arranged in such a way that one could see everything happening outside but no one could see in through the window, thus providing what I regarded to be blissful privacy.

I frequented this room every day for at least the first three years of secondary school. The vocational school had no facilities for making tea, and as my mother was fed up with me breaking flasks, I got permission from the principal to go down into town at lunchtimes. Others had similar permission, but I was the only one who went into Towey's. Perhaps the other students didn't know about it, and I never revealed any information about the place as I had made it my secret bolthole. I used to sit by the window eating the sandwiches I brought with me over Mrs Towey's cup of Irel coffee, which was only ten pence a cup.

Businesses were usually closed on Wednesdays owing to licensing laws, but Fair days, which were held on the second Wednesday of every month, were the exception to the rule. However, Mrs Towey allowed me in through her private side door when the premises were shut and used to make me coffee as usual. On these occasions I had the little room to myself. Fair days were in essence market days where traders set up stalls in the town's square selling clothes, household goods and furniture, and even some food items, including 'dilisk', a dark, salty, dried seaweed plant that was addictive to chew, often prompting me to ask my mother to buy some for me when I would meet up with my parents during lunchtime on Fair days. But on these occasions I often found my little bolthole in Towey's spoilt by overcrowding and my favourite table by the window taken by other patrons.

Fair days had a deep-rooted agricultural heritage attached to them with farmers taking along cattle, pigs, horses, sheep and chickens to sell. However, this practice waned during the early seventies when new legislation on cattle registration was introduced for farmers. Afterwards weekly cattle marts with licensed auctioneers began to operate in larger towns, although smaller farmers still preferred to take livestock along to sell at the monthly Fairs. Like all things associated with adolescence, I either outgrew Towey's or it outgrew me. One day the blinds were opened too much and my secret was unfortunately discovered. Some other boys from my school were walking past and saw me inside, and from then on, I got pestered by intruders coming into the room to satisfy their curiosity. It was never the same again and eventually I just stopped going there.

Upon arrival back from the summer holidays one year we were greeted with a new Maths teacher, Miss Naylor. I knew from the moment she arrived on Piper Hill in her blue Spitfire sports car that she was very different to any other teacher we had in the school. In one way everything about her was chic: she was in her forties, slim with a bouffant hairstyle and had a fast, elegant walk. But whilst she always wore different outfits every day, her clothes were sometimes of an odd mix. A pink skirt would be worn with an orange blouse with a frilled collar and, as with all her clothes, would be accessorised by a tight belt around her waist. Miss Naylor was a lady of both fascination and mystery. She had returned to Ireland after spending some years teaching in the Bahamas, and God only knew how her destiny had landed her on Piper Hill. She continuously filled us with stories about the Bahamas, the wealth of its islands, their beauty, the glorious climate, but she mainly spoke about the stream of famous people that came each year to holiday or who owned properties there. Miss Naylor had indeed seen many famous people and often dropped names at random – Princess Grace of Monaco, Elizabeth Taylor and Richard Burton, Audrey Hepburn, John Wayne, Jackie Onassis. These were apparently everyday sightings to her.

She became the fascination of the entire school. Different classes swapped stories about what she had said in their classes, and she was often the focus of conversation on the school bus home.

'What did she say?' 'Did she tell ye that she once met Muhammad Ali and chatted with him?' are examples of what was recounted.

With hindsight she loved to be distracted in class. She seemed a natural busybody who couldn't keep still as she walked around the class from one desk to another explaining the different equations in her lesson. However, there was little chance of actually learning Maths when her stories carried far more fascination than fractions ever could.

'Tell me more about the Bahamas, Miss,' was all one had to say and off she would go into a story.

But apart from her enviable past in the Bahamas, we knew very little else about Miss Naylor, other than that she rented a house in Tubbercurry. We never even discovered where she was actually from, whereas we knew far more about the other teachers – their spouses, children, where they lived, shopped and so on. She remained a constant enigma, riding around in her little Spitfire.

However, years later I was walking down a street in Galway when I bumped into her. She was incredibly charming as we recalled the vocational school until she completely lost me with her exclamation, 'All those mice!' According to Miss Naylor the vocational school had been riddled with mice, every classroom had them; they were under the floorboards and sometimes popped out from under the skirting boards when she was teaching. Personally, I had never seen a single mouse, let alone an infestation of them, in the six years I attended the school. Maybe there *were* mice in the school, or maybe Miss Naylor just had a terrific imagination. And just like the stories of the Bahamas, they might have been true or they could have been complete fiction. But even if fiction, they were very enjoyable nonetheless, and they served to ease the daily grind of Piper Hill.

Miss Naylor's sense of style unfortunately failed to rub off on Mrs Hegarty, our Irish teacher. She paid little attention to her clothes and certainly never wore any make-up. She maintained a distant attitude towards her students with a 'don't you dare mess with me' expression constantly written across her face, and she mainly referred to students by their surnames in Irish.

'MacEnri, have you done your homework?' she would ask me if she got the slightest inkling that an excuse was about to be offered instead of completed work.

Mrs Hegarty would never allow anyone to get away with any mischief in class and would quickly and sharply retort in Irish, *'eist a bhligeaird'* (listen blackguard). If her initial retort didn't frighten the perpetrator, then she would vent a tirade of humiliation at them in Irish in her loudest voice. But what stood out most about her was that she seemed to be forever pregnant. She was in her late thirties and generally had a baby every year, perfectly timed with the school calendar. Hence, each baby was born during the summer holidays, and then just before Christmas time, whispers and giggles would start again, indicating that there was 'another bun in the oven', to which I remember saying to other boys in my class, 'She can't be, not again?' Whilst there was no official sex education given in the vocational school, Mrs Hegarty's perpetual pregnancies were an education in themselves.

Despite Mrs Hegarty's commitment and vigour in the teaching of Irish, it remained a subject with which me and the other boys never became enamoured. Studying Irish in Ireland at that time was all about passing exams, so it wasn't unusual to be able to pronounce words correctly but still not fully understand what they meant. Neither was it uncommon to be able to write an essay in Irish and not be able to understand a conversation or to adequately translate a passage from a book. Each day my class used to take turns reading passages from *Breischeim*, an Irish short story book by Donnchadh O'Luasaigh. Whilst Mrs Hegarty frequently corrected us for mispronunciation of words she seldom translated any passages into English for us. I am not sure whether she expected us to translate them ourselves, but the truth was we often didn't have a clue what any of the stories were about.

Indeed, there were times at secondary school when I found learning Irish so difficult that I would have gladly given it up altogether. Then an opportunity presented itself that might have brought this about. It was during the summer of 1977, and Ireland was about to go to the polls in a General Election. Liam Cosgrove was the then Taoiseach and leader of the Fine Gael Party. The opposition leader was Jack Lynch from Fianna Fail. I was obviously too young to vote, but this didn't stop me from taking an eager interest in the political developments of the day. One of the election promises of Fine Gael was that if they remained in office they would abolish the compulsory learning of Irish in schools. However, Fine Gael lost, Fianna Fail got elected, and Jack Lynch became the new Taoiseach. Therefore, Irish remained on the curriculum, and I had to keep studying it. With hindsight, I am glad it did because despite my frustrations it clearly had great value as part of Irish culture and identity.

During research for this book I wanted to get a flavour of *Breischeim* and its stories and had parts of it translated. I discovered a lovely story about two young boys wanting to go to a concert, but they didn't have enough money to pay the admission fee. Then one of them came up with a clever idea about how to raise the necessary cash. Here is the story entitled *The Concert:*

> 'I would like to go to the concert in the hall tonight,' said Thomas to his friend Richard. '*The Bears* will be there you know. I just love their music.'
>
> 'How much is it to get in?' said Richard.
>
> 'Fifty pence,' said Thomas. 'But unfortunately I have only got eighteen pence.'
>
> 'I haven't even a penny myself,' said Richard. 'We'll have to stay at home, I'd say.'
>
> 'Ah, not at all,' said Thomas. 'We'll think of some way to make the money.'
>
> The boys walked to the end of the town. They stood on the bridge looking at the thin stream of water flowing slowly underneath. Now

and again, Thomas would throw a small stone in the water. No one spoke, each one thinking hard.

'I have it, I have it,' exclaimed Richard suddenly.

'What, what have you got?' said Thomas.

'A plan,' said Richard. 'Do you see that old piece of corrugated iron over there? Help me put it in the river here in front of the bridge.'

'But why? What have you got in mind?'

'You'll soon see what I intend to do,' said Richard.

They set up the piece of corrugated iron in front of the bridge. They placed large stones beside it to hold it steady. The water could no longer flow under the bridge and it was not long before a small lake had formed.

'Okay, away with us now to my house quickly,' said Richard.

'But you haven't told me your plan yet,' said Thomas.

'Look, give over and hurry up!'

Richard found an old discarded door at the back of the garage. He attached a piece of rope to it with a few nails. Then they went back to the river, and as they went Richard explained his plan to Thomas.

By this time there was quite a crowd of boys and girls looking over the bridge. The river was now like a small lake and they were all amazed. Richard threw the old door in the lake and it floated. He looked over at the people on the bridge. 'Look at the fine boat I have here, the Wild Seagull,' he said. 'I will give any of you a trip around the lake for five pence.'

'That's a great bargain!' But people were afraid to take a ride.

'Don't all rush in together, now,' said Richard. 'Five pence… four pence… three pence a trip!'

Nobody came forward.

'Here, Kathleen, a free trip for you!'

But Kathleen refused to sit in the boat. In the end, Richard himself went on board. Thomas grabbed the rope and pulled the Wild Seagull along the bank of the river to the end of the lake. He then crossed the river on stepping-stones in the shallow water. Then he walked along the far bank, pulling 'the boat' back to the bridge.

'Richard is back from the French Riviera,' said Thomas. 'Next passenger please!'

Then everyone wanted a ride but there was only space on the Wild Seagull for one person per trip. It was three pence for a single trip and five pence for two trips, one after the other. Everyone had great fun and some people wanted to have extra trips.

Who should walk across the bridge in the middle of the fun but Master Daly. He stopped for a while looking at the fun. Richard invited him to go on board. He did, but alas the poor man was too fat and the Seagull sank. The master went down with her, and he was soaking wet when he came out of the water. The 'boat' did not rise again nor indeed did the master's spectacles!

Thomas and Richard were very happy with themselves. It didn't matter that they would be in the master's bad books for a while; they had enough money to go to the concert!

One day our English teacher, Miss Williams, otherwise known as Celia because we used to refer to her by her first name behind her back, announced to the class that an Irish author by the name of Desmond Hogan was coming to our school the next day to talk about a book he had written. Celia, who was in her early thirties and single, had a moody personality. Her most striking characteristic was an unusual grin, especially at moments when she wanted to elicit a reaction from someone. It always seemed that she had more in mind than she was willing to say, and to provoke an acknowledgement from the class she grinned in this suggestive manner. That day was no exception with her saying, 'I wonder now what he'll be like', or words to that effect with a broad smirk during her announcement. She obviously knew some-thing we didn't and was looking forward to the thrill of what we would think of the author.

Desmond Hogan was very much a theatrical character. I remember him walking into classroom 5 dressed in brown corduroy trousers and navy tank top with the sleeves of his shirt rolled up. He stood at the top of the room with his back against the blackboard and in a loud and dramatic voice began reading from various parts of his book, switch-ing the book from hand to hand whilst he gestured with alternative hands on key points he was reading. It was hard to concentrate or to fathom out and understand the complex plot.

The opening words to Hogan's novel summed up the story quite adequately: *'This is a strange story.'* Indeed it was strange and to think otherwise would have been an understatement. Or at least those were my feelings back then when Hogan paid his visit to my class of fellow Leaving Cert students. Hogan was asked by the Arts Council of Ireland to travel around the country and do some readings of his debut novel *The Leaves on Grey*. This was a complicated love story between Sean, the main character, and Liam, whom he had known since childhood in Galway.

> When I speak of Liam I am speaking of a boy, beautiful, of a young man beloved by the women of Dublin, of a middle-aged man with a triad of expressions, adolescent, sage, nomad.

But it was more than a love story, even if an unconventional one, because it was complicated by the fact that Sean was also in love with Liam's mother, Mrs Kenneally, a Russian socialite. She committed suicide, but this didn't diminish Sean's thoughts about her. Indeed, such was his fascination for the woman that he couldn't figure out in his mind if he had actually physically made love to her at one point, so blurred had his infatuation become.

Hogan carried on and read out a description of Liam's appearance:

> Liam dressed in a long coat, slapped about him like a nightgown, a loose strap on it, a fall of blond hair on his forehead, eyes like the eyes of one partaking in espionage and lips that understood the smoking of cigarettes.

Hogan then gestured with his hands once again as he read out a scene of Sean losing his virginity:

> She came like a bird, wounded, frigid from pain, screamed a little. I pained her. I was the rugby player, the young athlete. She was the female, the object. I wanted to hurt her very much and she wanted the tenderness of hurt. She lay afterwards.

Hold on a second, I thought Sean was gay and in love with Liam. Well yes in a roundabout way. It was well documented to us that he was in love with Liam, an obsessive love by all accounts. But the word 'gay' was never mentioned. Confusing? It certainly was for a teenager trying to figure it all out. Whilst Sean had a strong emotional bond with Liam, there was no reference to them having sex together. The opposite, in fact, came across in Hogan's reading. When the story reached Dublin, where they were both university students, Sean slept with any girl Liam had previously been with. It became clear that anything Liam had, Sean wanted as well, and always seemed to get.

> When I returned from an outing with the mountaineering club, I
> found Liam and Sarah in bed together, this time without any qualms
> undressed to my underpants, I got in beside them, covered myself and
> some time in the night woke to find Liam and Sarah making love.
> That done I touched Sarah, her nipples, and her furze of pubic hair. I
> pulled towards her, roused into her, making love to someone who after
> all was just a nineteen or twenty-year-old girl.

I don't think anyone in my class expected Hogan to be so brazen in his reading, or that the book would contain such erotic references. The story progressed with Liam emigrating to Canada and Sean returning to live in Galway, where he married and fathered kids. Yet the lure of the past prevailed with Sean buying the house that Liam had grown up in. Sean and Liam continued to meet up every couple of years, trading stories before drifting their separate ways again, with Sean expecting their bond to continue for the rest of his life.

Hogan thanked the class for our attention before saying goodbye. I don't remember anyone, myself included, asking him any questions about his book. Shortly afterwards Celia returned after seeing Hogan to the exit. I can still see the grin on her face as she addressed the class. 'Well, what did ye think of that?' Nobody replied to her bait. God, she could be so vexing at times. Whilst she was a very good teacher, I was ambivalent towards her. One year she went to London for a holiday and when she returned she showed the class her holiday pictures. Some were taken in central London. She picked out one photo of Piccadilly Circus and the illuminations, to which she gave her usual grin before stating, 'And this is the area where queers and perverts hang out,' whilst looking around the room for any reaction from anyone in the class.

Thankfully the bell rang at that point, signalling the end of class. The renowned school cliché 'saved by the bell' that teachers delighted in espousing if a pupil encountered an awkward moment when answering a question was indeed at times a blessing. This time, the ringing bell meant escape from Celia and her prejudiced views.

7
Music was the Breath of Life

My childhood in Ireland in the mid-seventies can only be described as an era that consisted of music, dancing and singing. All of these were of course conducted within the boundaries of Catholicism, which were borne firmly in mind by nearly everyone. This was inevitable given the authority the church had in the country. The music scene and the lifestyle that went with it was like a revolution but, like all revolutions, it had a beginning, middle and an end. As a young child I joined its middle, continuing on to play a more involved role later in adolescence, before finally witnessing its decline.

Ceol is the Irish for music, and in the seventies *ceol* and more *ceol* fast became our way of life. The impact of country and western singers together with their showbands was simply quite extraordinary. It was as if the country had suddenly come alive after a long sleep and that exuberance was there for everyone to share and enjoy. England had the Sex Pistols, America was seeing the decline of Elvis, and Ireland was witnessing several singers gathering momentum, including people like Johnny McEvoy.

By the mid-seventies big showbands and singers were no longer confined to playing in cities and large towns and had disseminated throughout the country to nearly every rural part of the land. Johnny McEvoy was now at the peak of his career after making his debut with songs like *Mursheen Durkin*. Its chorus went 'Sure my name is Mursheen Durkin... and I'm sick and tired of working'. The song then went on to tell of a young man who went off to America to make his fortune – 'And instead of digging praties... I'll be digging lumps of gold'.

I was teased a lot about this song at home. My godfather, Johnny Durkin, took umbrage to this because of its name and loathed any mention or reference to it. It was unfortunate that his antipathy became so evident because my brothers constantly teased me about him and the song. I always fell for their bait by getting annoyed. Whenever Johnny passed our house on his motorbike, one or other of my siblings would duly deliver mutterings of 'Declan... Mursheen Durkin has just passed.' Ha ha, very funny indeed!

There were umpteen other singers and bands around at the time, including Joe Dolan, Philomena Begley, Big Tom and The Mainliners, Brendan Bowyer, Chips, The Conquerors, Red Hurley, Tweed, The Indians, Larry Cunningham, and The Swarbriggs.

The music scene in Ireland was generally split into three categories. One mainly consisted of Irish country music, which was greatly influenced by American country music. Irish artists did cover releases of American country songs and at other times combined American ideas into their own style of music. Secondly, Ireland also saw the growth of several successful pop bands and singers who wrote and sung their own material. Thirdly, there were traditional musicians who played what was collectively called 'ceili' music. This consisted of various musical instruments being played at the same time, including the flute, fiddle, piano accordion, bodhráns and the banjo, demonstrating great expressions of Irish culture.

As I mentioned in an earlier chapter, Irish society was changing as the result of a strengthened economy, but I don't want to paint a picture of great wealth because this wasn't the case. Emigration to England and America was still commonplace, but people did have a little more disposable income, which they primarily spent on music and entertainment.

Every great artist needs a place to perform, and the west of Ireland provided many artists with a choice of venues. Local towns had their own dance halls, and they were good enough to compete with those in larger towns and cities. In the early seventies public houses across the various counties in the west began to build extensions so that bigger artists could be invited to play there. It was at this point that, for the younger generation, an evening's entertainment comprised of two parts. For the first half of the evening there was entertainment and singing in the larger pubs and then, after closing time, people travelled on to dance halls for the second part of the night. There they would find bigger names from the music industry that would play until the early hours of the morning.

Kennedy's was a large public house just a mile and a half from our home. It was a very well-known venue because of its size and the music groups hired to play there. The proprietors had built an extension in the early seventies to make it probably the largest lounge bar in the whole of the west of Ireland. It had a very distinctive appearance with rust-coloured curtains hung over its black leather wall-to-wall seating, whilst tables and chairs were strategically placed throughout the centre of the room. The stage and dance floor were positioned to the right of the main entrance and in full view of the entire room. A full-length bar was situated at the far left of the lounge, and through the eyes of a child the lounge resembled a big square, but it was considered a posh big square at the time, and we felt so proud and lucky to have it in our locality.

Kennedy's was the place to be – and the place to be seen. Local bands played there mainly at weekends, and most of them were generally quite good. A few were out of tune, but this didn't seem to bother anyone. Dutch courage meant that the dance floor seemed to become the centre of attention and not the vocal chords of the singer, especially if a number came up which presented an opportunity for jiving. It was amazing to watch people do this dance because jiving requires attention to keep in pace with the dance routine. Some people were so good at it that it didn't matter if they had had a few drinks beforehand; they knew the dance routine by rote. However, other dancers were slow and had great difficulty keeping up with the rhythm.

Kennedy's also played host to many national singers and bands. On these occasions, there was an admission charge, usually either two or three pounds depending on the band or singer. My father paid little attention to music or singers and would often jokingly remark, 'I wouldn't go to see them if they were playing for free outside the back

87

door!' when he saw me or other members of the family going out to see these performers.

Johnny McEvoy was one of the star attractions to come to Kennedy's. He became a regular performer there, and whenever he appeared, people came from several neighbouring counties to see him. Hundreds packed the lounge bar as beer flowed and the air became thick with cigarette smoke. His concerts never disappointed because he had a terrific voice and delivered exactly what the audience wanted. The dance floor in Kennedy's was not terribly big, and this meant that if there were a dozen people or more dancing it looked full. Johnny's songs always enticed patrons out to dance. I particularly remember him singing *Grandma's Feather Bed*, an old hit record by the American singer John Denver. The song went like this:

> It was nine feet high and six feet wide
> and soft as a downy chick …
> It could hold eight kids and four hound dogs
> and a piggy we stole from the shed.

The chorus always ended with:

> We didn't get much sleep but we had a lot of fun on Grandma's
> feather bed.

The mid-seventies saw some amazing fashions for men, and this was as true in the west of Ireland as it was anywhere. All the shirts had big collars, then there was a brief phase of matching shirt and tie designs, and of course bellbottom trousers! The wider the better if you wanted to be considered truly fashionable. Platform shoes – how many inches? It was no good having platform shoes if someone else was going to overshadow you with bigger heels! Then there was long hair, and it was the fashion for younger men to grow it as long as possible.

Fashion for women was also at a turning point with the introduction of trouser suits, while others opted for dresses with short sleeves. Women's blouses, like the men's shirts, also had big collars. Some women were even brave enough to wear short miniskirts, but in the main they tended to dress conservatively or at least so in the west of

Ireland. Priests in Ireland were remarkably clever at linking the gospel reading to something emergent in society. Behaviour that implied sexual impropriety was quickly frowned upon, and the wearing of miniskirts was considered as immodest dressing. The clergy viewed it with the same disapproval as masturbation, homosexuality and sex before marriage.

Late night dance venues popped up all over the place, with the closest dance hall to us being the Central dance hall in Charlestown, County Mayo. When I was younger I envied my brothers being allowed to go to these dances, and I felt hard done by being the youngest in my family. My brothers were much older, which meant they went off to dances together whilst I had to stay at home. You had to be at least fifteen before being allowed to go to dances. Alcohol wasn't served in the Central because, like most other dance halls, it didn't have a licence. Beverages were mainly confined to non-alcoholic drinks like Fanta orange, Cidona or Pepsi. Instead, I had to be content with the news about the performers, which my brothers related to me the following day.

All the bands had printed picture cards of themselves, which they would distribute at the end of each night. My brothers were mainly pretty good at bringing these home – knowing if they didn't I would be disappointed. I collected the cards dutifully and pasted them together into a scrapbook along with cuttings from *New Spotlight* magazine, which was a weekly Irish entertainment magazine that contained news, gossip and features about national and international artists.

It is strange to recollect that when I wasn't allowed to go to these dances, I had such a strong yearning to go, but when eventually allowed I quickly ended up truly loathing them – it wasn't easy being a shy and timid teenager. I found these social gatherings stressful and not enjoyable in the least. The Central dance hall could easily have doubled as a cattle market, with its overall layout lacking any comfort. It would have been interesting to see it in the daylight, but few ever managed this. Instead, in its dimmed lights it gave a bare and drab appearance despite being filled on many occasions with several hundred people.

Men at these dances had to parade around the dance hall in between the dances to choose a partner from the lines of eager and not-so-eager females standing on the right-hand side. But some females had to endure the rejection of seeing handsome men pass them by and not ask them to dance. This was a two-way process of course, as some men got refusals and had to brusquely walk away feeling decidedly unwanted.

The Central dance hall was a bit of a Rocky Horror Show adventure really, in that it had the strangest mix of clientele. It had young gullible country teenagers witnessing a new phenomenon in life for the first time. Men in their twenties home on holidays from England who had pockets full of money, having spent the earlier part of the evening in the pub and were now out for a laugh and a good time. But the Central's main clientele were men and women in their early twenties anxious to settle down and marry. Here they could be found looking for their soul mates, with many finding them, or at least convincing themselves they had done so. And then there were bachelors and spinsters who, during their final days before middle age, were out desperately hoping to meet someone, anyone, they could marry. And then there was me. If I had lived in the era of James Joyce, this is probably how I would best describe myself within the remit of this experience:

> Now, should you pick up courage and ask a girl to dance or not? And if you do muster up enough courage, which girl will it be? Frankly, they all look much the same. Okay, you have to pretend that one of them stands out from the crowd and that she is the most gorgeous of them all. Pretending is an art, which you achieve with practice. Not every time though. Some girls have very high expectations and rather annoyingly turn their heads when the fox goes in for the kill. Unbelievably this may usually be a relief rather than a blow to your ego.
>
> However, round and round you continue to go pretending to look interested. At last, a girl accepts. She is not wearing spectacles but no

doubt suffers from temporary vision loss. Along with the acceptance to dance comes a multitude of dilemmas. How close should you get to her? What about your hands? Are these to be placed on her hips or lower back? Where do you position your head? This is a bigger problem than the positioning of your hands. You cannot get too close but on the other hand, you cannot strain back as if you are avoiding her face and neck. Ear to ear it is! Well, moderately so.

Then the song is over and hence a changeover of partners. Will you ask the girl to stay on for another dance without her getting the wrong idea? No, no, stop imagining that she will ask you to stay on. Then it happens... She wants to stay on the whole night. Does she actually fancy you? How on earth will you respond to this? Then before you have a chance to breathe, you have to place your hands in position again. The strategic closeness of faces also goes back into place as you boogie to another song.

Okay. People use each other in these types of situations and if you presume that it is anything else you could be in for a slap in the face. Some girls do not want to be wallflowers all evening and will dance with whoever comes their way. They are usually not the most attractive of female species, but they nevertheless possess a unique type of assertiveness which the prettier girls lack. They are not interested in kisses and meeting up again. Thank God for that you might think.

Hence, these girls are equally as devious as men ever are and will wait there at the end of the evening feigning innocence. What do you say whilst ending an agonising situation of this kind? Has it to be an outright lie? I really like you? Can we meet again next Saturday? You may of course be feeling inwardly 'I never want to lay eyes on you again'. You need not worry incessantly about the words which you are mustering up courage to say because girls of this ilk have the incredible intuition of standing and waiting to see their prey suffer and then, when you are about to mutter 'Good night – hope to see you again,' they will turn on their heels and flee from sight.

Dances were great fun for many people, and some even found lasting romance. But they weren't enjoyable for me. In fact, I found the best part to be home time after they ended at 2 a.m. It was such a blessed feeling of relief to know that I was returning to a safe environment and that the pressure of not being myself was over. I could take off the mask that camouflaged my shyness, awkwardness and insecurities in front of females in this type of social situation.

However, dance-hall scenarios as I have just described them were dying out by the late seventies. A change in the licensing laws meant that they were being phased out as hotels were offering better surroundings with the added bonus of being able to sell alcohol. The age of the nightclub and disco was beckoning, and this tended to put less pressure on shy reserved individuals like myself. The crude flamboyancy of dance-hall etiquette had been laid to rest, and no longer did social events in Ireland require women to line up waiting for someone to ask them to dance. New relaxed venues offered the opportunity to sit down and socialise with friends. I had lived through the dying days of the dance-hall scene in Ireland and shed no tears at their demise. However, I am confident that the resilience I deployed to get me through the experiences in Charlestown enabled me to build fortitude and develop the strength of character needed for challenges later in life. I can draw a breath in believing they had that value.

Father – a proud man on his tractor.

Haymaking in Derrykinlough with mother,
Padraic and father resting on the hayfork.

Father and John busy haymaking.

Father demonstrating his skill in roping a cock of hay, 1978.

*My father's beloved clock, inherited from his father, Thomas Henry.
It always drew compliments from visitors who admired its fine
handcrafted design. It hung on the wall in the sitting room, next to
the fireplace, with my bedroom close by. It was reassuring to hear its
tick-tock during the night or to suddenly wake up and count its
chimes, never knowing for sure whether some were miscounted or not.
It also loved to interrupt, especially during 'Dallas' when it
demanded full attention as it chimed the higher hours of the evening.*

*Aunt Annie, Padraic and mother taken
at the Rooskey community games 1977.*

Mother, father and Aunt Annie enjoying the games.

My parents looking happy, taken
outside the front door in Derrykinlough.

Me. What a pose!

Teatime in the hay field with me in between my parents.

Kevin taking a break.

*I'm perhaps a little overdressed for the hayfield,
but it was a photo opportunity after all!*

Mother and I in her Ford Escort car, summer 1978.

*Marie and Nora in fine fettle in Nora's house in Brackloon
(alas, Nora passed away shortly after this was taken).*

*I went to Knock to see the Pope but failed in my mission!
Sunday 30th September 1979.*

Undoubtedly me!

Veronica with father who is smoking his pipe.

A sultry and smouldering look! Galway awaits me.
September 1981.

8

Events to Amuse, Entertain and Occupy

The main musical entertainment on television during my youth was undoubtedly the annual *Eurovision Song Contest*. Watching *Eurovision* was as much a part of my life as school or haymaking. Unmistakably frivolous, it was escapism from the more banal events of daily life. This was life at a time when there were no mobile phones, computers, iPods, game consoles, satellite or high-definition television. Every year I watched it, hoping, almost praying, that the Irish entry would win. Before this I eagerly watched the *National Song Contest* on RTE, the Irish television channel, to see which entry would be chosen to represent Ireland at *Eurovision*. I was very patriotic concerning the Irish entries irrespective of whether they were any good or not. The year 1978 stands out particularly when Colm Wilkinson represented Ireland in Paris with a song he had written himself entitled *Born to Sing*. I was glued to my seat in the sitting room at home watching Wilkinson, the first artist to perform that evening, come out on stage dressed in a navy velvet suit, consisting of a bomber jacket with a long white silk scarf tied and draped over his front. He was undoubtedly the best singer to have sung for Ireland in *Eurovision* and perhaps it may not be an exaggeration to say that he was the best singer to have performed in *Eurovision* itself. His voice was captivatingly powerful that night. *Born to Sing* was an up-tempo number and told the story of the singer's itinerant lifestyle, and how he missed his lover who did not want to travel with him, and his destiny by being a man born to sing.

Here are two verses of the song:

> Some day, I hope, you will understand why I live this way
> Songs keep moving in my head, this music I must play
> So I pack my bags and once again I get out on the road
> Another day, another night, I might catch my soul.

And a man is born to do one thing and I was born to sing
And I must take the good times and the bad times that it brings
And I missed you in the morning but most of all at night
And I couldn't stop the music, but I tried with all my might

But alas the song only managed to get fifth place out of the twenty countries performing that year, with Israel eventually winning, to my incredible disappointment. Unfortunately, nobody at home relished Colm Wilkinson with the same fervour as I did. So it was no surprise when my brothers refused to go with me to see him perform at Teach Murray's – a public house in Gurteen – when he was touring Ireland in the months following his appearance at *Eurovision*. On the day of his performance in Gurteen I was with my mother driving home from Boyle, another small town reasonably close to our home, when we were met by a car travelling in the opposite direction. I recognised the driver at once to be Colm Wilkinson and instantly felt star-stuck at this unexpected sighting. I couldn't help thinking how he would be singing *Born to Sing* hours later so close to where I lived and I wouldn't be going to see him perform. So near and yet so far! Soon after this he left behind the pubs and dance halls of Ireland and went on to international stardom, starring in a string of successful musicals, including leading roles in *Les Miserables, Jesus Christ Superstar* and *The Phantom of the Opera*.

But not all Irish representatives at *Eurovision* found success like Colm Wilkinson. In fact, most of his predecessors only had five minutes worth of fame before disappearing back to playing in often dank local venues around the country. We watched the attempts of singers like Maxi, Sandie Jones and Red Hurley come to nothing. Then there was Tina Reynolds, unforgettable maybe for her singing but not for the white dress she wore on the night of her *Eurovision* appearance. It was ahead of its time with its low-cut, off-the-shoulders design, combined with an opening at the stomach area, which revealed even more flesh. This was 1974 and what a tough year to be in the contest because onto the world stage stepped Abba, representing Sweden with *Waterloo*. But I wasn't sitting in Derrykinlough cheering on Abba; instead my focus was on my Irish Waterloo, namely Tina, who sang *Cross your Heart*.

> Cross your heart say I love you,
> Cross your heart and hope to die
> For a very simple reason and here's the reason why,
> For so many hearts are broken by one little lie,
> Cross your heart and hope to die ...

Afterwards the chorus went *La La La La La La* for at least fifty times, or at least it felt like that many. The disappointment of Tina not winning prevailed for a little while before the excitement of Abba took hold. They were quite simply a spectacular music sensation the like of which the world had never previously experienced – dressed as they were in their elaborate costumes and platform shoes. They dominated the music charts month after month, year after year, with me buying every single one of their records.

Other memorable competitors at *Eurovision* were the Swarbrigg Brothers – Tommy and Jimmy. They were long-established Irish singers – renowned for their long hair and check bellbottoms. Both were in their early thirties when they represented Ireland in Stockholm in the 1975 contest with *That's what Friends are for*. They were dressed in matching sky blue polyester suits with large lapels and wide trousers. It was a terrific ballad, but to my incredible disappointment it only came ninth in that year's voting.

> And when troubles full and plenty,
> Come piling at your door,
> That's what friends are for.
> Ladies and gentlemen of the whole wide world,
> If every now and then,
> A single voice was heard.
> Telling it like it should be, making it simple and plain,
> If that man needs a helping hand,
> Help him in from the rain.

Then two years later in 1977, they were chosen for a second attempt, but on this occasion they were accompanied by two female singers under the name 'The Swarbriggs Plus Two', singing It's Nice to be in Love Again. However, such was the insignificance attached to 'Plus

Two' that I never bothered to discover the names of the two girls – it was obvious their purpose was merely padding for the performance. The spotlight instead remained with the brothers, this time dressed in matching polyester black jackets with large sequined lapels and white trousers. But they had to settle for third place after getting beaten by France who won and the UK who came second.

By 1980 my disappointment had nearly dried up because my interest waned after both the Swarbriggs and Colm Wilkinson's attempts at winning had failed. I thought that if they couldn't win, there would be little hope of victory for anyone that followed, but I was in for a shock. Johnny Logan, a singer I had never heard of before, was chosen to represent Ireland with a ballad entitled *What's Another Year?* What made the song unique for me was the fact that it was the first time I had ever disliked an Irish entry. It was a nostalgic song about getting over pain and loss I am not quite sure whether I experienced horror or delight when Logan won. Delight maybe that he had put Ireland into a positive limelight by winning, and horror that the song was so dull. The song went:

> I've been crying such a long time,
> With such a lot of pain in every tear.
> What's another year for someone who has lost everything
> that he owns?
> What's another year for someone who's getting used to
> being alone?
> I've been praying such a long time, that's the only way to
> hear the fear,
> What's another year?

But Logan's dress sense made up for the bland tune. He was a good-looking man, and for the contest he was dressed in a white suit, black shirt with a black silk scarf. His ostentatious dress sense didn't stop there though. At a later appearance on *Top of the Pops* when the song reached number one in the UK charts, he sat on a stool as he sang, with his jacket draped over his shoulders without anyone questioning his sexuality or labelling him gay. But he managed to bring a fresh and welcome perspective to the Irish male fashion scene.

∽

Irish television during the seventies mainly consisted of imported American serial dramas and detective series. There were some home-made programmes, but I regret being critical when I say that these were mainly quite dull. *The Riordans,* a weekly soap opera about rural farm life was set in County Wicklow. It wasn't necessarily a badly made programme, but it played safe with its storylines, hence there was seldom any controversy with its characters. Controversy in the seven-ties would undoubtedly be nothing more than a woman having a child outside wedlock. *The Riordans* certainly didn't do rape, murder or vio-lence. What about a gay character? There wasn't a chance in a billion of this happening in the still staunchly Catholic Ireland of the 1970s because it would have caused a public outcry. Instead we had to be content with Mary, one of the central characters, cooking for her farmer son, Bengy, his favourite dinner. A cow calving with twins brought a little excitement, as did the village curate, Father Sheehy, dropping into the Riordan household for his weekly chat over tea, which would be served in Mary's best china tea set.

Hall's Pictorial Weekly with Frank Hall was a comical yet sometimes wry political satire. Ireland was always a very politically inspired coun-try, so watching a programme like this about the politicians serving a country immersed in recession was boring for a young person to watch, hence my viewing of it was quite limited.

Mike Murphy was a well-known Irish presenter on both television and radio, and his variety show *The Likes of Mike* saw him carry out candid-camera-type pranks on members of the public. He used to dress up using several disguises and catch people out, and they were totally unaware they were being tricked. Later on he did another series called *The Live Mike*, and it was on this programme that Dermot Morgan (later to star as Father Ted) made his debut as a comic. Ironically he played a priest in this as well, playing Father Trendy, a comical Roman Catholic priest who attempted to draw nonsensical parallels between the Bible and everyday Irish life. An example of this included him comparing the parable of the six loaves and fishes to how people would need to economise following a national budget. Sometimes the jokes were funny but at other times they were only mildly humorous.

Gay Byrne was also a stalwart of Irish television and radio. *The Late Late Show* on television was mainly a chat show for celebrities and guest panellists discussing controversial topics of the day. Byrne once interviewed a journalist from *The Irish Times* newspaper; the discussion was about religion and the Pope. I recall the journalist making some harsh criticism to Byrne about Pope Paul VI, saying that he was too old for office and out of touch with society, particularly concerning the Vatican's stance on divorce, contraception, homosexuality and sex before marriage. I remember being rather vexed at his audacity at criticising the Pope, to whom as a trusted young Catholic I had pledged my allegiance. I thought the journalist's point of view was horrible at the time, but if it was now I would probably be watching and agreeing with him.

So in absence of quality homemade television we watched a plethora of American programmes. Who could forget *The Streets of San Francisco* with Michael Douglas playing Steve Keller, the handsome young detective, along with the veteran actor Karl Malden? *Macmillan and Wife* with Rock Hudson and Susan Saint-James. *Charlie's Angels,* three glamorous private investigators played by Kate Jackson, Farrah Fawcett-Majors and Jaclyn Smith. *Columbo* in his old rain mack, which starred Peter Falk, never failed to trip up the most articulate murderer in his investigations. Just when I thought that the culprit had been clever enough to escape justice, Columbo would find the missing link and solve the crime. I sometimes wanted programmes like this to end with the police failing to catch the murderer because in real life, their record of catching them wasn't so plausible. Then there was *Magnum PI,* set in Hawaii, which starred Tom Selleck. I watched this mainly to see the amusing eccentric quirks of Higgins, played by John Hillerman, who demonstrated perfect aristocratic Englishness. Both Magnum and Higgins oversaw the estate in Hawaii of a wealthy author, and both were from military backgrounds but had totally opposite personalities. Magnum's carefree lifestyle was in total contrast to the elegantly spoken, dressed and etiquette-prone Higgins.

We were fortunate enough to receive Ulster Television (UTV) in our house thanks to a special aerial which my parents had erected, which meant we were able to watch a wider variety of programmes, including English sitcoms and soaps, many of which were not shown on RTE. However, sometimes there was a crossover between RTE and UTV to the airing of American or English programmes. It was therefore not impossible to have seen an episode of a particular programme on one channel, only to discover it being shown another night on the other channel. However, it was the norm for all TV channels to close down transmission every night at around midnight during the seventies.

I doubt if a Sunday went by when an episode of *The Little House on the Prairie* wasn't aired on either RTE or UTV. The weekly highs and the lows of the Ingalls family were played out on their little farm in the 19th century American west, starring Michael Landon in the lead role as Charles Ingalls, namesake of the author Laura Ingalls Wilder, whose book was adapted for the programme. Likewise, I also watched *The Adventures of Black Beauty*, every weekend. I adored this classic story, which was based on Anna Sewell's novel, and which featured the dramas of Dr James Gordon, played by William Lucas, and his children, showing the intuition and kindness of Black Beauty in each programme. Another favourite was *The Partridge Family* with a storyline set in California about a widowed mother and her five children who were all embarking upon a family music career. David Cassidy played the eldest son in the family, Keith Partridge, who with his chiselled good looks, beautiful long hair, talent as a singer and guitarist, used to make me watch and wish I was a member of the Partridge family too! Other programmes included *The Sweeney* with hard-man police portrayals by John Thaw and Dennis Waterman. The quirky and oblique *The New*

Avengers with its secret agents and bizarre storylines starring Patrick Macnee, Joanna Lumley and Gareth Hunt.

Comedies on UTV included *Man about the House* and its spin-off *George and Mildred* both starring Yootha Joyce and Brian Murphy as an ill matched married couple. There was the famous Benny Hill, who never failed to raise a laugh with his special brand of silliness, sexism and drag acts. *Bless this House* starring Sid James, who played a hapless father of two lazy, layabout children in their early twenties who constantly sponged money from him. *Love Thy Neighbour* about two families, one black and the other white, who lived next door to each other. This was a comedy with both husbands, played by Jack Smethurst and Rudolph Walker exchanging banter and name-calling, which would nowadays be considered offensive and racist. However, it was acceptable in the seventies to use words like 'Nig Nog' and 'Honky' within the remit of humour. I had never seen a black person whilst I was growing up in Ireland and was oblivious, as most other people were, that these words were racist and discriminatory.

I was reared on a diet of *Crossroads* and *Coronation Street*, the two main British soap operas of the day, but I preferred *Crossroads* out of the two. Just as fans of any television serial soak up the drama and intrigue of its characters, I did so in a zealous way with *Crossroads*, which was set around a motel in a fictional country village called Kings Oak in the English midlands. Perhaps in my subconscious I would have liked Derrykinlough to have been like Kings Oak and have the tranquil shops, mainly the village teashop that was depicted in the programme. The storylines in *Crossroads* were about loyalty and family affairs, which were perhaps quite similar to some of the day-to-day situations that most people and families have to face, with the exception that being a television programme, the conclusion to each scenario invariably produced idealistic outcomes, rather unlike real life.

Television in the seventies produced its fair share of camp actors. But the style of humour had a covert edge to it and the comical routines of the characters fell short of identifying their sexual orientation. There were Kenneth Williams and Charles Hawtrey in the *Carry On* films, and John Inman in *Are you being served?* Comedians and game show hosts included Larry Grayson, Dick Emery, Frankie Howerd and Kenny Everett – all of whom received their fair share of curiosity in relation to their sexual orientation. Society was content with quietly guessing but would quickly disapprove if anybody revealed that they were in actual fact gay. This would have been considered an aberration that conflicted with the religious and moral beliefs of Ireland. Therefore, any interest in the subject had to be kept secret.

A massive scandal hit the headlines in the late seventies that intrigued me from start to finish. This was no ordinary scandal because it was a love affair between two men. A love affair that had gone bitterly wrong and resulted in a kind of trial that the Old Bailey in London hadn't seen for a long time. Indeed, many would say it was a type of trial that the world hadn't perhaps witnessed since the tribulations of Oscar Wilde.

Jeremy Thorpe, who was leader of Britain's Liberal Party, was on trial for conspiracy to murder Norman Scott, a former male model. Allegedly Thorpe and Scott had been lovers in the early sixties when homosexuality was still illegal in Britain. Then almost two decades later Scott started to divulge information about their 'love affair' to a tabloid newspaper. He showed the *Daily Mirror* love letters that Thorpe had allegedly written to him at the time of their affair in which Scott was addressed as 'Bunny', a pet name that Thorpe created for him.

Every afternoon after school I used to buy the *Evening Herald* in Vera O'Toole's newsagents before catching the bus home. I devoured every detail of the trial such was my fascination at the drama of it all. I hated the name 'Bunny' and thought it a ridiculous nickname to call a man.

Thorpe was accused of conspiracy to murder and for inciting a paid assassin to murder Scott in order to silence him from leaking more information to the media. Apparently, the assassin had almost succeeded in carrying out the murder. One day when Scott was out walking his dog, the assassin came up to him, took out a revolver and shot Scott's dog dead. The assassin then pointed the gun to Scott's face but luckily the trigger jammed.

Thorpe's trial was the main headline on every bulletin on the UTV news. Every evening I watched the early evening news that followed *Crossroads*, taking in every word the newscasters reported on the latest developments in the trial.

The defence claimed that whilst they had once been friends their association didn't comprise of any sexual element. They cited black-mail threats as the reason and claimed the murder allegation did not hold any foundation of truth. The jury believed Thorpe and acquitted him of all the charges. However, his political career was unable to withstand the scandal of the trial and he resigned shortly afterwards as leader of the Liberal Party.

But the drama of *Crossroads* and the intrigue of the Thorpe trial could never have prepared anyone for the wealth and grandeur that the TV series *Dallas* was set to provide. The launch of *Dallas* in the late seventies was as much a phenomenon in Ireland as it probably was elsewhere in the world. Everybody watched *Dallas* in Ireland, and everyone talked about *Dallas* in Ireland. It was everyone's dream to be surrounded by the wealth the characters in the programme enjoyed. Looking back now, I can see how my contemporaries and I, from the rural west of Ireland, would have been fascinated by the affluence of the Texan oil industry. However, when I now reflect upon this I can appreciate how wealthy people, like those portrayed in *Dallas*, would yearn to escape from their particular pressures to the beauty and simplicity to be found in the Irish countryside. It is possible to visualise envy on both sides, with each culture yearning to have what the other had – whilst never truly appreciating what they themselves possessed. *Dallas* was broadcast late on Monday nights, and by late I mean after 10 p.m., which meant that it was not over until after eleven at the earliest. This entailed me staying up late to watch it. I wouldn't have been able to face school without having seen it the night before, other-wise I would have risked being lost in conversation, as *Dallas* always featured prominently as the main topic amongst my peers every Tuesday morning.

In addition to *Dallas*, two other favourite programmes of mine were also American. *Hart to Hart* starred Robert Wagner and Stephanie Powers, and the storyline was about the Harts and their butler Max, played by Lionel Stander, living a jet-set life in California. But despite their wealth the Harts spent most of their time playing amateur detectives getting entangled mainly in cases of murder, hence the opening words to the title tune narrated by Max:

> This is my boss, Jonathan Hart, a self-made millionaire, he's quite a guy. This is Mrs H., she's gorgeous, she's one lady who knows how to take care of herself. By the way my name is Max. I take care of both of them, which ain't easy because when they met it was murder.

It was easy to envy the character of Jennifer Hart, a freelance writer, married to a millionaire, seeing her seated in her study in their luxurious Californian home, tapping away at her typewriter with shelves of books in the background. It all seemed idyllic to me as I sat at home in Derrykinlough absorbed in daydreams.

Then there was the *Six Million Dollar Man*, played by Lee Majors, who also happened to be dashingly handsome. Like *Hart to Hart* there was a little story spoken in the opening titles after we were shown the horrific crash which badly injured poor Steve:

> Steve Austin, astronaut. A man barely alive. Gentlemen, we can rebuild him. We have the technology. We have the capability to build the world's first bionic man. Steve Austin will be that man. Better than he was before. Better, stronger, faster.

I did wonder at the time if such a large amount of money would be spent on Steve if he wasn't so attractive. Week after week we were treated to seeing him catch and destroy criminals in his role as a secret agent working for the American Intelligence Bureau. He never flustered when using his amazing bionic strength or when his implants got damaged. Neither, amazingly, did his hair get ruffled as he ran at speeds of up to sixty miles per hour.

∽

Not much seemed to happen in our local community except for the entertainment which Kennedy's provided but the music scene in pubs waned in the late seventies with fewer big names appearing and much smaller audiences as a result. Recessionary times had hit Ireland once again. The time had come for new ideas and for a new regeneration of our community.

People were uncertain about what would really work but eventually came up with the idea of building a community centre. It was thought that this would provide a means of entertainment to local young people and provide a form of community cohesion to the locality. However, the only problem behind this idea was that the parish didn't have enough money in its coffers to fund building it. Had the school building in Derrykinlough been preserved after it closed eleven years before, this might have provided the solution. But the building had long since been demolished, and therefore in order to raise funds for the proposed community centre Rooskey Community Council was formed in 1977.

I recall a local elderly woman describing the idea of people gathering funds to build a community centre as ludicrous. Perhaps she feared that it would turn out to be another 'white elephant' just like the ball alley in Rooskey had become. This was built in the late 1960s at a time when handball, a Gaelic sport similar to squash where players hit the ball at high speed with a hand instead of a racquet, was a national sport in Ireland. But interest in the sport decreased in the late sixties, leaving the ball alley deserted. The old lady sarcastically said the locality already had two community centres, referring to the two local pubs, and scornfully enquired why there was a need to build a third one. It was difficult to argue against her point because the temporary base for the community centre was set up in the rooms attached to Benson's, the pub located in the heart of Rooskey village. Irish people have long been associated with an image of being heavy drinkers, and what the old lady said appeared to reinforce this belief because socialising from the temporary community centre spilt over to the bar next door on some occasions. However, this facilitated the experience of meeting people and socialising, as opposed to being unduly exposed to under-age drinking.

A variety concert was one of the first ideas mooted to raise funds for the development of the community centre, and I was enticed to sing in this. In the beginning, I went along with the idea because I sang a lot when younger and believed myself to be a good singer. However, the choice of song was a terrible mistake. Looking back on it now, I think the person who encouraged me to sing *Blanket on the Ground* should have been hung, drawn and quartered (metaphorically speaking of course!). It was a parent of one of the younger participants who encouraged me to take to the stage. She may probably have thought if I practised more I would make the grade.

In fact the song now brings a smile to my face when I remember its lyrics. An Irish singer, Philomena Begley, did a cover version of the song, originally by Billy Jo Spears, the American artist, and because of its lyrics it is obviously better sung by a woman. In fact, it is difficult to imagine a man ever singing it. Here is the chorus to the song for you to judge for yourself:

> I'll get the blanket from the bedroom
> And we'll go walking once again
> To that spot by the river
> Where our sweet love began
> Just because we are married
> Don't mean we can't slip around
> So let's walk out by the moonlight
> And lay the blanket on the ground.

What do you think? Could you picture a man singing it? Well, I need not have worried about singing before a live audience because the concert was cancelled anyway. I think the reason for this was insufficient material and participants to produce a full show. This no doubt saved me from much embarrassment and teasing from by broth-ers. The concert was substituted with a quiz evening and raffle. I got placed on one of the teams for this and prepared myself by thinking about possible general knowledge questions that I might get asked.

On the evening of the contest something extraordinary happened. As I went into the bar by the side door I was approached by a familiar figure. I shall refer to her as 'Mrs Delaney', and she was a tall, elegantly dressed woman in her sixties. She was wearing her usual large spectacles and had a walking cane, which rested on her right arm like a fashion accessory.

'Can you escort me into the bar, young man?' she said to me.

It was more of a command than a request from this enigmatic character. I may have muttered 'Okay' back to her because I was so dumbfounded by the task I had been asked to carry out. I took hold of her left arm and gently walked her along the short passageway and took her to the bar, where a special stool was reserved for her. She made a grand entrance. I had seen Mrs Delaney several times before and knew that she was a character in her own right. She, on the other hand, didn't have a clue who I was, but this didn't matter to me, for she had made an impression on me through the mystery and fascination that she projected.

Mrs Delaney placed herself on a barstool as usual, and this was where she normally held court whilst sipping a gin and tonic and smoking a cigarette in a cigarette holder. Laughter echoed from her direction as she conversed with some of the regular patrons. The interesting part of her modus operandi was how she kept a caring and watchful eye on the bar regulars who appeared to be drinking too much. Her commands of 'Steady on there, Caffrey,' 'Steady on there, Jennings' or whatever the person's surname was, were usually met with respect and with an instant alteration in the person's behaviour and drinking. This was in recognition of the admiration and fondness in which she was held.

My team lost in the quiz, which was a slight disappointment at the time – especially as there was a little cheating with some people whispering answers. Perhaps if Mrs Delaney had not been so engrossed in conversation at the bar, she would have made an excellent and elegant adjudicator – which would have been quite advantageous to these social fundraising events.

Enthusiasm continued in securing funds for the new community centre with low-key events like the quiz evening and the annual community sports day, which was held each summer. However, by the time sufficient funds were secured and the community centre was built, it was too late to be of use to my generation. Unfortunately, another white elephant had come into being, just like the old woman said. The generation after mine didn't take to it either. Times had moved on, and apart from the occasional social event it largely stood idle and closed. Society had become more advanced with the age of the disco and nightclubs arriving for older teenagers whilst the younger ones had simply declined in number.

I was very excited when I visited Dublin for the first time with my mother in August 1977. This was a couple of weeks before returning to school, and we travelled to Dublin by train from Ballymote. This was also my first time travelling on a train, and I felt like I was going on this amazing voyage to a distant, faraway country, even though it was only a three-hour train journey from Ballymote to Connolly Station in Dublin. We were visiting Kevin, who had been stationed as a *Garda* (policeman) in Dublin the previous year after he had completed his police training. My mother and I stayed in a hotel in the city centre and visited Kevin in his flat in Ranelagh daily.

My first impressions of Dublin were favourable. I loved the buzz of the place and had never before seen so many people or so much traffic. A whole new horizon opened up right before my eyes. The shops were fantastic, and I loved the items they were selling. Being a typical teenager I loved clothes and found a great selection in every store. Seeing the city's wide streets with pavement newspaper vendors was not something I had experienced in the local towns of County Sligo, and I remember taking lots of the most ridiculous pictures of buildings and streets in an attempt to capture the atmosphere of an exciting first visit to the capital of Ireland, which I thought was an eye-opener. I also found an extensive range of records and tapes. Along with some purchases of Abba and Bee Gees records was a Lena Zavaroni LP. Thinking about this now makes me squirm, but at the time I was a huge fan. Buying her records at a bargain price simply added to my large record collection. I had enjoyed her cheekiness with the TV host Hughie Green a couple of years beforehand when she made her debut on *Opportunity Knocks*, singing *Ma, he's making eyes at me.* Yes, of course, I had voted for her. In those days, telephone voting was unheard of because basically not everyone had a telephone, so the only system of voting was by post. *Opportunity Knocks* was broadcast every Monday night on UTV, which meant that you had to act fast or else your postcard would not arrive on time. The post in those days took ages to get from Ireland to England. It was a case of racing on my bicycle – or getting my mother to dash in her car – to the local post office every Tuesday and post it so that hopefully they would get the postcard by the following Monday. It probably never arrived on time, but at least I had pacified myself in believing that I had voted for my favourite artist and had contributed to his or her win, including Lena, of course.

I loved BBC Radio 2, and we received an excellent airwave reception in County Sligo. My favourite DJ was David Hamilton. My taste in music was diverse and I even liked The Bay City Rollers. I doubt many people would actually admit to that now, although they sold 120 million records over the course of their career! Equally I was able to appreciate the extreme opposite and had become a fan of the classic folk rock band Lindisfarne when they released their single *Run for Home*:

> I've travelled the land,
> With a guitar in my hand,
> And an eye ever open for some fun,
> I've made some mistakes,
> Had my share of the breaks,

Seen the boys on the run and on the bum.
Run for home run as fast as I can
Oh-oh running man ... running for home
Run for home run as fast as I can
Oh-oh running man ... running for home.

One Sunday evening when I was listening to the Top 30 it was announced: 'And the number one record this week is – *You're the One that I Want*, by Olivia Newton-John and John Travolta.' There I was practising with a hairbrush and miming my hardest with the radio almost on full volume. I had this amazing position in the sitting room where I would pretend that the mat by the fireplace was a stage. It was a large rug so this made things a little easier. We had this big picture of a lake and wood scene on the wall over the television, which faced me. Irrespective of whether the light was on or not, the reflection in the picture was enough to satisfy my ego. I helped invent karaoke as I sung and mimed to my heart's content. Of course, if my mother or one of my brothers walked in, I would instantly stop and pretend I was doing something else. I fail to understand any teenager of my generation who saw *Grease* and didn't dream of having a part in the film. It was certainly the feel-good factor of the late seventies, along with John Travolta's other classic dance film *Saturday Night Fever*.

Vincent Hanley was an up-and-coming radio and television presenter who had his own late-night show on Irish radio. I really liked his voice and style of presenting, so I decided to write him a complimentary letter and requested that he played David Soul's song *Silver Lady* on a particular evening. I loved this song and couldn't get its words out of my head. I was in Brackloon visiting Marie on the evening that I requested the song to be played and nearly forgot about it. Then I suddenly remembered and had to hurriedly cycle the three miles home in order to be in time for the beginning of the programme. I hadn't bargained on so many midges being out, but it was a balmy evening, and I was soon covered in them. My haste meant that I didn't have time to visit Aunt Anne, my mother's widowed sister who lived in Cloonlairn, the village next to Derrykinlough. Her house was en route to

Brackloon so I nearly always paid her a visit either going or on my way home. Aunt Anne was very humorous, like my mother, and there was always lots of laughter during our *shanahes* (conversation consisting of humorous gossipy tittle-tattle and news items). Other times we would sit and watch television, and every time she never failed to single out some character in a programme and make a remark along the lines of 'Look at the face of that one' or 'Big mouth' and mimic whoever caught her attention on the screen. But there was no time for a visit that particular evening.

I got home just in time to set up my cassette player to record the programme before it started. It was marvellous hearing my letter being read out on radio, my name being mentioned, and Vincent thanking me for my nice remarks about him. Hearing *Silver Lady* being played enhanced the occasion even more. Let me give you a taste of the song:

> Come on Silver Lady take my word,
> I won't run out on you again,
> Believe me, Oh I've seen the light,
> It's just one long fight, without you.
> Here I am a million miles from home,
> The Indiana wind and rain cut through me,
> I'm lost and alone
> Chilled to the bone,
> Silver Lady.

Songs from the Bee Gees, along with David Bowie, Abba, Billy Joel, Leo Sayer, Queen, Supertramp and Electric Light Orchestra dominated the charts at this time. Whilst BBC Radio 2 was definitely my favourite music station – RTE launched a new radio station in the late seventies. This was the first national station within Ireland to play pop and rock music continuously throughout the day. It was trendy and chic, and new pop and rock-mix groups began to form. Ireland saw the formation of The Boomtown Rats with Bob Geldof, and U2 with Bono, who both made their debuts around this time. However, neither of these groups surpassed my liking for Bagatelle, a group of four men from Dublin who had a massive number one hit with *Summer in Dublin*.

It was a simple ballad with beautiful harmonious music sung by the band's lead singer, Liam O'Reilly.

Take me away from the city and lead me to where I can be
    on my own,
I wanted to see it, and now that I have, I want just to be left alone,
I'll always remember your kind words, and I'll still remember
    your name,
But I've seen you changing and turning, and I know that
    things won't be the same.

I remember that summer in Dublin, and the Liffey as it stank
    like hell,
And the young people walking on Grafton Street, and
    everyone looking so well,
I was singing a song I heard somewhere, called Rock'n'roll
    never forgets,
When my humming was smothered by a 46A and the scream
    of a low-flying jet.
So I jumped on a bus to Dun Laoghaire, stopping off to pick
    up my guitar,
And a drunk on the bus told me how to get rich. I was glad
    we weren't going too far.

So I'm leaving on Wednesday morning trying to find a place
    where I can hear
The tunes of the birds and the sea on the rocks, where open
    roads always are near,
And if sometimes I tire of the quiet, and I want to walk back
    up that hill,
I'll just get on the road and stick out my thumb. I know that
    you'll be there still.

What made the song so appealing was that it told a simple and direct story. It was a compelling song with an aura that almost invited people to think of cherished memories from their past. And that is what I have done here, share precious memories from the seventies with you. I am sure a lot more happened in the music and television worlds back then than I have recalled, but these are the parts that stayed in my memory as the events which amused, entertained and

occupied me during my adolescence – and it is for this reason that
have shared this selection of anecdotes with you.

9

And Then there were Three

I was sixteen when Padraic died in a horrible accident in Edinburgh during the Easter of 1979. He had left Ireland the previous year to work as a mechanic on a large construction site on the outskirts of the city. Owing to a long-running postal and telephone dispute in Ireland at the time, we had not heard from him for several weeks before he died. My parents half-expected him to pay a surprise visit home over the Easter holidays, and they even considered going to Ballymote train station on the Saturday to see if he had come home on the evening train from Dublin. Little did any of us realise that at this point he was in the last few hours of his life.

Padraic was living in a mobile home on grounds close to the construction site where he worked. He had been out socialising with friends in Edinburgh on Easter Saturday. It had been a very cold evening, and it was assumed that when he got home the mobile home would have been chilly. Apparently he switched on the heater and the gas cooker to warm the place but had become drowsy from the warmth and fallen into a deep sleep. He was never to wake up again, as Padraic died of carbon monoxide poisoning. The following morning when a friend called to visit him he found him dead.

Easter Sunday delivered the first sight of good weather after a long and bleak winter. The gloriously bright and sunny day brought with it a temperature well in excess of what was normal for late spring. It even felt warm in the shade. Neil Diamond was number one in the charts with *Forever in Blue Jeans*, and I was enjoying being off school for the Easter holidays, especially so because that year I was studying for my Intermediate Certificate with exams pending in May and June. We had gone to Mass as usual, and it was around the time that we arrived home that Padraic's body was discovered in Edinburgh, but it would be another thirteen hours before this terrible news reached us.

There was a band playing in Kennedy's that night, and I joined my parents there for an evening's entertainment. We returned home at 10.30 p.m. and had something to eat before going to bed. I was awoken just after midnight by a loud knocking on our front door. I could see and hear the lights and the engine of a car running outside our front gate from my bed. Then I heard my mother getting up to answer the door. Next, I heard a man's voice talking to her, but I could not hear the conversation in its entirety, just the occasional words and phrases here and there. I pieced these together sufficiently to realise that Padraic had been involved in an accident. I heard my mother bravely ask the man if her Padraic was dead, and he replied, 'Yes.' I jumped out of bed and immediately went and woke John. I remember shaking him whilst shouting, 'Padraic is dead, Padraic is dead.'

I went into the sitting room dressed in my pyjamas, where my mother and the man were talking. My father joined us very shortly afterwards. The deep shock had rendered us numb with disbelief. There was no way that we had remotely expected such pain and grief to descend upon our lives. Whilst attempting to take in the enormity of the news, we were jolted by the behaviour of the driver accompanying the man talking to my mother. Becoming impatient at waiting, he beeped the horn of the car several times. His insensitivity surpassed anything I had ever previously experienced, but at the same time it was ignored due to the trauma suddenly thrust upon us.

The days between receiving the news of Padraic's death and his funeral saw dozens of neighbours, friends and acquaintances calling at our home to offer their condolences. Irish people on the whole are very kind and sympathetic people. The greater majority of the callers were genuinely upset that Padraic had died and gave heartfelt words of comfort, but some people have a tendency to recognise a vulnerable moment and seize upon it. Hence there were a handful who literally interrogated my parents about the circumstances of Padraic's death, wanting to know everything down to the last detail. Then there was the woman who appeared more interested in our home than in anything else and enquired of my mother how many bedrooms were in the house. Her curiosity went even further when she asked who slept where. In an effort to make light conversation another elderly visitor from the neighbouring village spoke about the method by which he remembered to take medication for his heart condition. Every night before he went to bed he prepared his tablets for the next day by placing two tablets on the kitchen table to remind him at breakfast time. He put another two tablets on a saucer by his radio to take when the Angelus played at noon. Then a further two tablets by the clock on the mantelpiece, which prompted him to take them after it chimed five o'clock. I hated people calling at our house; I was shy and wanted to withdraw from them and their sometimes idle conversation. We hardly had any time alone to talk amongst ourselves, and besides, they were putting too much stress and strain on my parents.

John and Kevin flew to Scotland midweek to deal with the formalities for the return of Padraic's body to Ireland. I stayed behind with my parents to help them as much as I could with the funeral arrangements. My father was simply too distraught to go along with my mother to meet the cemetery caretaker and choose a burial plot, so I went with her instead. From the choices available we decided on a plot that was raised up on a slope, with a little valley and boreen road beneath. There was something about this location that inspired tranquillity, making it a good choice.

Padraic's body was flown from Edinburgh to Dublin on the Thursday after his death. My parents, Aunt Tess and I travelled there together. The driver collected us early that morning, as the journey to Dublin would take four hours, including a meal break. The flight was due to land in the early afternoon, actually arriving shortly before we reached the airport. John and Kevin had travelled on the same flight as Padraic's body, and after meeting them, we were all taken to a private chapel in the airport where his coffin had been placed.

There is something final about seeing a coffin because when you see it, you fully realise that a person is truly dead. The carbon monoxide poisoning had damaged the upper part of Padraic's body, and the authorities in Scotland advised my brothers that it would be too distressing to see his body, so therefore instructions were passed on to the undertaker for his coffin to remain sealed. Funerals in Ireland have stuck to a rigidly held tradition down through the decades and are in two parts. It is customary for the bodies of deceased persons to stay overnight in their local church prior to burial, with evening prayers recited upon the arrival of the body. The burial then takes place the next day after a funeral Mass.

An entourage of friends had travelled from Edinburgh to attend Padraic's funeral. Friends and neighbours from our local area had also driven part of the way to Dublin in order to meet and follow the cortège back home. When we arrived in Derrykinlough the undertaker stopped the hearse outside our house as a customary gesture to say a final goodbye. This was painfully poignant, knowing that this was the closest Padraic would ever get to being inside the family home again. It was at this moment that the reality of his death really took hold. Members of the local community had arranged a guard of honour. Several dozen men of various ages were lined up in pairs wearing white armband sashes, with sets of six men at a time taking it in turns to carry his coffin for the last mile to the church. Evening prayers at St Joseph's church in Rooskey were scheduled for 10 p.m., but it was nearly eleven by the time we arrived. Vast crowds of people came to the funeral that night. We were all emotionally exhausted but had to carry on with the task of being greeted by long queues of people extending their condolences. At sixteen, I was simply overawed by the whole experience.

Padraic's funeral Mass wasn't held the next day but on the Saturday instead owing to the late arrival of his remains to the church on the Thursday evening. So the next day we went to visit Padraic's coffin in the church. It was a quiet and private time for us and perhaps the first time since he had died that we could grieve together as a family and in private. During this visit I noticed there were brown tassels draped at each corner of the coffin, making it look different from Irish coffins and that it also had a beautiful cross on it.

For the funeral Mass I was dressed in a navy blue cardigan, which my mother had bought for me in McGovern's in Gurteen, matched with a navy shirt, black tie and black trousers. I still have a clear visualisation of my parents, brothers and I sitting in the front pew of the church, which was filled to capacity with relatives, friends and neighbours. Father Flynn, the parish priest offered comforting words. The school choir sang *The Lord is my Shepherd*. The coffin was blessed with holy water and fanned with incense smoke from the same thurible that I had so often struggled to light, years earlier when I was an altar boy. The guard of honour was formed again half a mile before the cortège reached the cemetery. The men took it in turns once more to carry Padraic's coffin for the final few hundred yards until they reached the cemetery gates. It was then time for the family to take over. My father, my brothers and I then carried the coffin to the graveside. The coffin felt unbearably heavy on my shoulder, and I felt guilty for feeling relieved once I was released from the burden.

Images of Padraic accompanied me everywhere after his death. I often imagined that I saw him in different places for years after he died. It was not unusual to be on a bus and for someone a few seats in front to resemble him from the back. Then the person would get up and from their side profile, it would become quite obvious that it wasn't him. The same thing happened in town sometimes when a person walking in front triggered a likeness. The compulsion to get near to the person and identify with the resemblance was often intense. Then I went through a phase of believing that he wasn't really dead. I almost convinced myself that it had all been a mistake and that he would come home one day. All sorts of scenarios went through my mind. How would the family deal with this? How would we explain it to people? Perhaps believing this was because I had not seen Padraic's body after he died, therefore I imagined he had not really died. I thought that anyone could have been in the coffin, hence fuelling my fantasy that his death had been a mistake. In many ways, this illusion was a comfort, but it came with a price. The price for me was years of not fully accepting that he was dead.

The impact of Padraic's death had ramifications for all the family, but especially for my parents. I remember one occasion a few months after he died when my father was working in a field half a mile or so away from our house. This field was probably the nicest field on the farm because it had a stream adjacent to it. Dinner was ready and my mother asked me to go and tell him. I remember walking up the pathway that led to the field and seeing him. I could see the pain etched all over his face as he rested his hands across the shovel he was holding. A discussion about Padraic's death suddenly found its rightful place. Here was my father, a man who had worked hard all his life to provide for his wife and sons and was now faced with the most traumatic experience that a parent could endure – the loss of a child. We just talked and talked, going over the pieces of information which had been passed on to us from sources in Scotland and attempting to rationalise what might have been changed if the circumstances surrounding Padraic's life had been different. My father hadn't wanted him to go to Scotland, as he felt uncomfortable about the job and the living conditions. He also I guess felt protective towards Padraic, who had a lucky escape the year before he left home. He was involved in two separate motorcycle accidents, with one of them so serious that he had to have emergency surgery to release pressure on his brain, such was the extent of his head injury. My mother too went through her own personal anguish. She was immensely brave, and it was she who kept everything in the family ticking over. On one occasion, some weeks after Padraic's funeral, I recall seeing her do something that I had never seen her do before, smoking a cigarette with Marie. It was clear that her sorrow was deeply intense.

A short time after Padraic's death some visiting missionaries came to our parish. One of the American priests in the group had given some warm and humorous sermons at Mass and I felt drawn to him. I came home from school terribly upset one Friday evening, and as I knew he was going to be hearing confessions in the church I decided to cycle to the church to see him. I noticed the church was empty when I arrived. I entered the confessional box and burst into tears whilst telling him that one of the female teachers at my school told my mother on a parent-teacher evening the night before, that she thought I had got over Padraic's death rather quickly. My mother disliked the teacher and thought what she had said to be horribly untrue. What angered me most was that the teacher had never even spoken to me about Padraic's death. She had never once asked me how I felt or if I needed help, and therefore she could not have had the faintest idea of my feelings. Inwardly, I had to bear the injustice of the teacher's comments because I hadn't the courage to go and challenge her on what she had said. The priest was kind and reassuring and explained that the teacher had no right to be so judgemental. It was such a relief to receive his warmth and understanding at a time when I felt so emotionally vulnerable.

The summer of 1979 was, in the main, uneventful; we just went on with our daily tasks as best we could, including the usual round of turf and haymaking. However, one significant event did occur on a hazy, warm day in late August whilst we were haymaking in Brackloon. It was on Monday August 27th, my parents wedding anniversary, when we heard on the news that the IRA had assassinated Lord Mountbatten in Mullaghmore, County Sligo. This picturesque seaside town where Lord Mountbatten had his holiday home, 'Classie Bawn Castle', was only about forty miles away from my home. I recall this incident in particular because it was one of the rare moments when my family felt ashamed to be Irish. This cowardly act of terrorism had supposedly been carried out in the name of all Irish people, but that was simply untrue. We had never spoken to, or indeed known any Irish person who would have advocated such barbarity against English people. Before the murder I must admit I knew little about the Mountbatten family or their connection to the British Royal family – but I felt loss and revulsion nonetheless that he was murdered in such an horrific way.

Re-adjustments took time to get used to, and Christmas 1979 saw only my parents and myself at home. Kevin was working in Dublin, and John was away in London. The place was full of memories of Padraic's presence the previous year, not least with his birthday falling on December 22nd. We had even gone to some of the dances in Charlestown together the Christmas before. In a real sense a part of the family unity, the thing that held us together, had cracked. Padraic's death had fragmented the family unit; it could never be the same again, and neither could any one of us.

With Padraic being the closest brother to me age-wise I connected with him more closely. A prime example of this was when I wrote a letter to *St Martin's Magazine* and it got published. I was depressed with the world one day and decided to write to the question-and-answer page bluntly enquiring 'Why do you think people are thick?' I was absolutely thrilled that it got published because all my previous attempts had failed. I had often frantically written telling them, through my wonderful and vivid imagination, that several murders had been committed in Derrykinlough and that the murderer remained at large in our community and then asking, 'What is Ireland coming to – allowing this sort of thing to happen?'

Here is the winning attempt in getting published – my letter to Question Box and the magazine's reply:

> I am really fed up with thick people. They seem to be everywhere these days. I would like *St Martin's Magazine* to answer my question 'Why do you think people are thick?' **Declan Henry, Co. Sligo**

> You don't explain what you mean by 'thick'. It could mean someone who has missed out on an education, or it could even mean someone who doesn't agree with your point of view. I'm sure you realise that some people are more intelligent than others, and in any case we all have different talents. Our Blessed Lord Himself made allusion several times in the Holy Gospels to the lack of belief and lack of understanding of His apostles, but He was patient with them and they eventually achieved great things. Perhaps you could follow His example when you come across someone whom you perceive as being 'thick'. **St Martin's Magazine**

I remember showing the magazine to Padraic. He was amazed but also highly amused that I had written to the magazine's editor with such a question. Since my mission had been achieved with my name in print, I wasn't too bothered about the reply. My ego was doing over-time. I felt that I had well and truly made my introduction as a writer. We both had a great laugh about it!

10

The Pope's visit to Knock

As a child, annual trips to Knock were as synonymous with summertime as were trips to the seaside. But this small religious village in County Mayo held a mystery attraction like no other place because it is here that Mary, the Mother of God has appeared. Therefore, it was considered a very special place to visit, not least because it has, alongside Lourdes and Fatima, become one of Europe's major Catholic Marian shrines.

It was on the wet Thursday evening of August 21st, 1879, just after 8 p.m, when the Blessed Virgin Mary, accompanied by St Joseph and St John the Evangelist, made her two-hour apparition in front of fifteen people, including men, women, teenagers and children. She was dressed in white and golden robes and wore a crown on her head. She appeared to be praying and had her hands and eyes raised towards Heaven. My grandfather, Thomas Henry, would have been just five years old at the time of the apparition, and I have often wondered what he was doing at home in Derrykinlough, which is just fifteen miles away, on that great night, and what fascinating stories he must have listened to in the aftermath of the apparition. The apparition took place just thirty years after the Great Famine. Perhaps it wasn't a surprise that such a distinguished divine figure appeared in Ireland, bringing comfort to a populace that had seen much disease, death and mass emigration, particularly in Mayo, one of its poorest counties.

Although Knock was relatively close to home, a car journey there as a young child seemed like a long journey. I remember travelling to it in a minibus one hot summer's day with my mother, with Padraic and I squashed in the back seat. There was always excitement when arriving in Knock and seeing row upon row of stalls lined up either side of the main street selling religious memorabilia. This naturally created a very different scene to what I was used to seeing in Ballymote, Tubbercurry or even Gurteen. Medals, rosary beads, scapulars, prayer books and bottles of holy water were almost compulsory essentials to buy during trips to Knock. I also remember one time getting a toy camera that revealed a series of images pertaining to the apparition when the shutter was clicked. It was utter simplicity but undoubtedly would have kept me occupied on the way home in the minibus.

The big new basilica in Knock, built in the autumn of 1976, received a lot of media coverage, as it was the biggest in Ireland. My father was particularly anxious to see it, and sure enough we made the trip the following summer. Kevin drove us in his car to see this majestic new building that covered an acre of land and had a seating capacity of ten thousand. I thought it was massive inside, and I had never been in such a large building before, let alone a church of this size. Afterwards we went for a walk around its outside ambulatory. It didn't go unnoticed to my young eyes as we strolled around this covered walkway that there were green plaques placed in a row on the upper wall of the pillars with the names of the thirty-two counties of the four provinces of Ireland, Ulster, Munster, Leinster and Connaught, individually recorded. I observed that the plaques were not in order or grouped together according to the provinces, except for Ulster, where the six of its nine counties that formed Northern Ireland were in a straight line – Derry, Antrim, Down, Fermanagh, Armagh and Tyrone. The remaining twenty-six counties were all mixed up, which perhaps engendered a little more interest whilst keeping an eye out for Mayo, Sligo and Roscommon, as well as also looking out for some other counties in Ireland that I had visited. Apparently, the main reason the plaques were displayed was because stones from each county had been used in the building of the basilica.

In 1979 the biggest thing to happen in Knock since the apparition occurred was the arrival of Pope John Paul II. The Pope's visit to Ireland was the second biggest news story that year after Lord Mountbatten's murder. The fact that it came the month after the murder made a welcome and positive change to the news bulletins. His visit was to mark the occasion of the centenary of the apparition of Blessed Virgin Mary, and everybody in Ireland was very excited about his visit. His first year in office had shown him to be different to his predecessors, and he was willing to travel around the world and be accessible to his people. He was far younger than previous pontiffs and was handsome and masculine with a down-to-earth approach that really endeared him to the Irish people. Thousands of people from all over the country and world flocked to Knock on the day of His Holiness's visit, not least because it was the first time a Pope had ever set foot on Irish soil. I too was in Knock at that time, but my recollection of the occasion was far less fascinating than the accounts portrayed in the media. In fact, the whole experience was simply bizarre. I did not see the Pope at all despite being in Knock for several days before his visit, and there was a reason for this.

The vocational school had arranged with local scout leaders in Tubbercurry that students from the school could travel with the scouts to see the Pope. The boy scouts were younger than us, and as a result we had little in common with them. However, we shared a common goal, and that was to see the Pope. We set off from Tubbercurry two days before his arrival in order to take up our positions, as massive crowds were expected to descend upon Knock.

Being part of the boy scouts' entourage, our accommodation in Knock was in small tents, each sleeping four people. I had never slept either in a tent or in a sleeping bag before, nor have I slept in either since. After setting up the tent for the night, it became apparent that there was no toilet or wash facilities on the campsite. It was either 'do your toilet' behind a tree or walk a mile and a half to the village where there were toilets close to the basilica. I decided on the latter every time. Despite the campsite's lack of amenities, there was a real buzz of excitement in the adjoining fields where a platoon of soldiers was also camping. It was fascinating to watch them in their green jumpers and commando trousers as they were young, fit, handsome, and entirely enviable. They would not have been cold either because the smell of their open campfire was tangible in the air. I envied them having hot meals around the campfire, especially as my diet in Knock consisted of snacking on biscuits, chocolate and chips.

The nights seemed endless in the tent as a mild frost formed outside, and despite being fully clothed, sleep only consisted of brief interludes before the cold woke me up again. Whilst there is undoubtedly a peacefulness and sanctity to be found in Knock, the grey, damp and misty weather on the weekend of the papal visit didn't enhance the atmosphere, but there nevertheless was an air of silent excitement as the place prepared for the head of our church to come and visit this humble Irish village.

Seeing His Holiness would undoubtedly have made up for the misery endured in Knock, but it just wasn't meant to be. My friend Dermot and I spent a lot of the time in the village centre except on the day of the Pope's visit; which was exactly where we should have been on that day. On the day of the visit, Dermot and I decided to play it safe and to remain near the campsite. The Pope's route was marked out and the organisers had intended that he would journey around the main perimeters of the adjoining fields of the shrine in the Pope-mobile. A good opportunity would hence be given for all to see the Pope close up. All that was necessary was for me to have my camera at the ready in order to take some excellent photographs. We thought we had devised a clever plan and would get a once in a lifetime close-up look at His Holiness.

On the day of his visit to Knock, the Pope presided over another Mass in Galway, thirty miles away. This service unfortunately overran, which resulted in him arriving late in Knock. Large cheers and hand-clapping erupted when the Pope's helicopter finally touched down. Dermot and I watched as the Mass was celebrated. The Pope could be seen as a little red dot near the altar on the platform, which was specially erected for his visit. This is how it appeared to us from three-quarters of a mile away where Dermot and I stood. I took photographs, which mainly captured the backs of people in the large crowd. The red dot which represented the Pope came out even smaller in the photos and resembled no more than a tiny speck of red ink left on a piece of paper by the tip of a pen.

As the Mass was drawing to a close, the heavy mist turned into a light rain, resulting in the evening getting darker sooner than usual. This brought about a very disappointing conclusion to the Pope's visit because his security advisers cancelled the proposed journey around in the Pope-mobile. Dusk had brought things to a halt as His Holiness's advisers gently ushered him to his helicopter for the trip back to Dublin, where he was staying.

Dermot and I stood and watched the helicopter rise high into the sky as it left Knock. For a moment we were dumbfounded that the Pope had left, and that we didn't get an opportunity to see him. Shortly afterwards the rain became heavier. Reality sunk in that I had tolerated the place for two days completely in vain. Then regrets instantly began to flood through me. I was really disappointed that we ended up in a situation that could have been avoided. On the other hand, it was deeply embarrassing, and we wished we had been more adventurous and gone into the crowded village that day and pushed our way to a prominent position close to the altar. I don't believe that I admitted to my parents or to anyone else who knew I was in Knock that I hadn't seen the Pope. Lies were inevitably told. 'Oh yes, I saw him… It was wonderful seeing the Pope,' I replied when asked!

The evening spent walking around Knock after the Pope's departure and standing on the platform where he had celebrated Mass hours earlier didn't make up for the bitter disappointment of not seeing him in person. Furthermore, another damp and uncomfortable night had to be endured in the tent, but the regret of not seeing the Pope began to fade and was soon replaced by thoughts of going home to proper food, warmth and a hot bath – all of which were joyously craved. The fields around Knock were emptying again, with only litter left behind as a reminder of the invasion of the preceding days.

I bought a mug with the Pope's portrait on it, as a souvenir. This along with the obscure photographs was all I had to commemorate the momentous occasion. And so we set out to make our journey back to Tubbercurry with a combined sense of exhaustion yet relief that it was all over. Let no one ever say that it is easy being a Catholic!

11

Time to Move On

The summer before I left secondary school I worked in a public house in Ballymote. I cycled each day to a neighbouring village, where I met up with a friend, also named Declan. He then gave me a lift in his car to Ballymote, where he too worked. He was slightly older than me, but we both shared the same great sense of humour. The pub I worked in was a clean and well-organised family-run business at the bottom of the main street and belonged to a man named Batty Cawley. Batty and his wife Eileen looked after me well, providing me with £15 in weekly wages, including meals. Working in Cawley's was my first taste of independence, and the first step towards really growing up. It was also an exciting challenge that helped to boost my self-confidence. I loved working in the bar, where my days were spent meeting a mixture of people who I thought were intriguing, but were in fact more often than not just ordinary and humble people who either lived in the town or came from the local country area.

There was occasionally an odd character or two who visited the bar and I took the opportunity of writing about one of these customers in a school essay when I returned after the summer holidays. The following is an extract taken from my religious education exercise book, entitled *Why Priest?* I imagine this vague title was meant for students to write about the merits of priesthood, but I seized upon the opportunity to write about a priest I had served one day in Cawley's.

> During the summer holidays, I worked in a pub. One morning my
> first customer was a priest. I took particular notice of him. He was

* This was in reference to a priest in America who I had read about in a newspaper.

127

very impatient and gave me the impression of being neurotic.

After pricing nearly everything in the bar, he decided upon buying a bottle of Scotch. Whilst I was getting him his change from the till, I noticed that he had gone to the far end of the lounge. He was trying to hide something behind the radiator and this something was an empty bottle of vodka, which he had taken out from the inside of his raincoat. He changed his mind and came back to the counter and handed me the empty bottle to put into the rubbish bin, took his change and was out the door as fast as the wind.

Believe me – this priest had a hangover and a drink problem. It's a disgrace to see a priest with a drink problem and even more disgusting to see a priest drunk as I have in the past. If these priests are so near to God in their prayers why doesn't He help them overcome their drink problems? Indeed, priests are like everyone else: Sinners! What about the *priest who was involved in a bank robbery last year? I am sure he wasn't robbing the bank to get money to build a new church.

My idea of a priest is a good living, hard working person who is prepared to do good for his church and its people – to set good examples and not be crazy for money as some priests are, to be friendly and helpful to people who have problems, not proud and carefree, etc. Many priests don't practice what they preach.

As a young boy, I said I would be a priest but not now. I feel any young man going into the priesthood nowadays is taking on a big challenge. I doubt if this challenge is ever fulfilled. Do you agree?

I must point out that the foregoing were the mutterings of a teenager and were, perhaps, dramatised to provoke a reaction from the teacher as opposed to a reflection of what I genuinely felt. Any intentions of the kind may have backfired because, if my mind serves me correctly, I think the assignment remained completely uncommented upon. However, the story remained true in part, and I can still picture the priest trying to hide the empty bottle of vodka behind the radiator.

My parents wanted me to have a trade after I left school and urged me to consider toolmaking as a career. For my part, this filled me with dread. Although I went to a vocational school where the usual pathway led to training in some apprenticeship or other, I secretly harboured ambitions to be either an actor or journalist. Indeed, I often wrote off for prospectuses for such courses without my parents' knowledge. I think if I had to fault my parents in any way, it would be for having sent me to a completely unsuitable secondary school where I perceived myself as being a misfit for six years. Nevertheless, I had no alternative but to accept this mismatch as best I could.

I was invited to an assessment and interview at the Regional Technical College in Sligo for toolmaking during the summer holidays of 1980. This was to secure a place on the following year's course. I could not avoid going, as this was what my parents wanted. I decided not to argue with them and instead secretly hatched a plan that I would go along to the assessment but would sabotage my chances of ever becoming a toolmaker. Therefore, on the day of the interview I wasn't the least bit nervous. Before the actual interview I had to sit some awful aptitude tests that consisted of multiple-choice questions where you had to choose what came next in picture sequences. This was great as it allowed me to give the wrong answer every time. I was hoping to get every answer wrong and would have been most disappointed if I thought I had inadvertently given the correct answer to any of the questions. Then I was called for the interview, which, alas, was not destined to run as smoothly as the aptitude tests. It is one thing feigning ignorance on paper, but when put in a face-to-face situation it is much harder, as I was to find out. There were two men interviewing but only one of them asked questions, whilst the other just sat and listened. I was asked several questions – 'Why do you want to become a toolmaker?' and 'What skills are needed for the job?' and so on and so forth. During these questions the most astonishing thing occurred. I could no longer pretend to be stupid and started answering the questions to the best of my ability. The whole process was being reversed and I remember leaving the room completely dejected thinking my plans had been foiled. I thought they would offer me a place on the course, leaving me no option but to become a toolmaker.

A couple of weeks later I received a letter from the college with the dreaded result. I opened the envelope fearing that my plan might not have worked but instantly felt a great sense of relief and freedom when I read the immortal words 'It is with regret that we have to inform you that you were unsuccessful in the assessment for the toolmaking course.' Then the letter went on to say that they were willing to offer me a place on the 'fitter' apprenticeship course instead.

Thankfully my parents renounced their wishes for me to study for any apprenticeship because they needed no persuading to convince them I would have been completely unsuitable to undertake training as a fitter. Their rationale lay in the belief that toolmaking was considered a clean job – in contrast to being a fitter, which inevitably would have meant lots of oil, grease and dirty overalls. Would this have been me? No was the only possible answer to that question. I think that learning any kind of mechanical or technical apprenticeship requires a deep interest, coupled with a desire to learn more about a particular subject. I certainly didn't possess any yearning to study for an apprenticeship, and besides, I never overcame my secondary school fear of working with machinery, all of which would have made me a lousy apprentice.

I eventually decided to go on a one-year City & Guilds food and beverage course at the Regional Technical College in Galway. This decision was made with great difficulty because in the months prior to completing the Leaving Certificate, I was almost clueless as to what I really wanted to do with my future. This was owing to a combination of drawbacks that resulted from receiving inadequate career guidance at secondary school, and being at a school which was ill suited to my personality and general personal development. I owed the deciding factor to Declan – the friend I mentioned earlier. He had attended the same course the previous year and recommended that I apply for a place.

I was delighted when I passed the interview for the course a few months later. The interview was on a Thursday in Ballymote and my father was going to the Mart in the town that day; he kindly offered me a lift on the tractor. However, apart from it not being an attractive mode of transport, my father was a very slow driver, and I am sure it took us two hours to complete the ten-mile journey.

The interview itself was mostly an informal discussion, as opposed to questions and answers, about food and hospitality etiquette. However, the interviewer did ask me one question that stood out from the rest. He explained that it was necessary to be good at giving directions when guests asked for them before asking me to give him directions to the nearest supermarket in the town. Anyone who knows me well knows that I am hopeless with directions and hence a rather poor navigator. But I rose to the occasion and in quite a convincing tone, bluffed my way with directions on how to get to Keans supermarket.

> If you take a left turn outside and continue on before turning right at the bottom of the road, continue on for two hundred yards and then take another left turn at the bottom of the hill, turn the corner which leads you onto the high street, and there on your left-hand side you will find a supermarket named Keans.

What I had told him was complete nonsense. Thankfully he wasn't from the local area and therefore remained unaware of my deceit. Indeed if he had heeded my instructions, he would more likely have landed himself in the middle of a field full of cattle rather than finding his way to Keans in the town centre!

After the interview I walked to the cattle mart to join my father. He decided that we should go and have lunch in a nearby restaurant before setting out on our journey home. I still remember the meal we had – roast beef, turnip, peas and mashed potatoes. There was no dessert available so we finished the meal off with tea and rich tea biscuits; surrounded as we were by farmers discussing cattle prices and other agricultural topics.

∾

A couple of months before I was due to sit my final exams I fell ill with chickenpox. I had to take time off school to recuperate, but during my recovery I tried to keep busy practising for my looming oral Irish exam. When I returned to school, my face was full of spots and holes, but this did not prevent Mrs Hegarty from duly reprimanding me for not having studied hard enough.

'MacEnri – how on earth do you hope to pass your exams with the little amount of effort you're putting in?' she enquired.

She then set about instructing me to tell the examiner that I was recovering from *Bolgach Naionan* (Irish for chickenpox) in the hope of extracting a little sympathy from him for my health problem. I remember announcing this to the examiner, trying my best to make a good impression. It must have worked as I ended up passing the exam.

There weren't many students doing the Leaving Certificate that year as numbers in our school had steadily dwindled over the previous few years. In fact, I can only recall four other boys completing their schooling at the same time as myself – Dermot, Benedict, Michael and Eamonn. We got on as a group mostly, but none of us kept in contact afterwards and I have never seen any of them since. The subjects I took for the Leaving Certificate were English, Irish, Mathematics, Business Organisation, Agricultural Science, Mechanical Engineering and Technical Drawing.

A week before the exams started, the priest who taught us Religious Education, Father Eugene Duffy, decided that he would hold a Mass in the school for the Leaving Certificate students. There were two reasons for this. The Mass was intended to help us with the pressures of the impending exams, and also to act as a goodbye and good luck gesture for our future. The Mass was held in the wooden prefabricated building at the back of the school in what was called classroom 10. The desks were tidied away for the Mass and a makeshift altar was erected. There were fewer than ten people present, which included some of the teachers. During his address, Father Duffy talked about the upcoming exams, but also drew our attention to an unlit candle on the altar. Lighting the candle, he reminded us that it would serve symbolically as a beacon to those present ending secondary education with the intention that hope, guidance and protection would remain with us on our respective journeys. The simplicity of this candle and its message has always remained with me when recalling that Mass in that small wooden room. The image of the lighted candle is still vivid. There was something mystical about the candle and the words Father Duffy used to describe how the light the candle represented would go forth and be with us for the rest of our lives.

∽

The summer of 1981 culminated in the lavish wedding in July of Prince Charles to Lady Diana Spencer in London. But the months preceding this momentous occasion saw an assassination attempt on Pope John Paul II in Rome and another on President Ronald Reagan in America. In the weeks leading up to me finishing secondary school Buck's Fizz won the *Eurovision Song Contest* in Dublin and the death of the IRA hunger striker Bobby Sands took place in Belfast. His death on the May 5th received international media coverage. I, too, listened to endless news reporting on his hunger strike, which lasted a total of sixty-six days in the H blocks of the Maze-Long Kesh prison in Belfast, situated a hundred and thirteen miles from my home in Derrykinlough. The significance of mentioning the mileage lies in me wanting to draw attention again to the two different worlds of Ireland. Even during the early eighties it seemed impossible that peace would one day belong to Northern Ireland because death and mayhem continued there relentlessly on a daily basis.

The aim of Sands' hunger strike was to regain the 'special category' status for republican prisoners, which had been removed. They wanted to be identified as political prisoners, separated from other prisoners, and have no prison uniform or prison work. Sands had already served one prison sentence and had, by the time of his death, completed five years of a second fourteen-year sentence for terrorist crimes. Before Sands went on hunger strike, he and other republican prisoners took part in protests, which saw them refusing to wear clothes, opting to cover their bodies with blankets instead. They also refused to wash and would rub their excrement on the walls of their prison cells. The following is an extract from Sands' journal, which was leaked out of the prison:

133

> Dear God, another day, I thought, and it was far from a pleasant
> thought. Naked, I rose and crossed the cell floor through the shadows
> to the corner to urinate. It was deadly cold. The stench rose to remind
> me of my situation and the floor was damp and gooey in places. Piles
> of rubbish lay scattered about the cell, and in the dimness dark, eerie
> figures screamed at me from the surrounding dirty, mutilated walls.
> The stench of excreta and urine was heavy and lingering. I lifted the
> small water container from amongst the rubbish and challenged an
> early morning drink in a vain effort to remove the foul taste in my
> throat. God, it was cold.

My life couldn't have been in greater contrast to that of Sands' self-
imposed predicament. I used to wake up every morning with the birds
singing in the trees across from my bedroom window in the clear May
blue skies and hear my mother in the kitchen, knowing that it would
only be a matter of minutes before she would arrive at my bedroom
door to announce that it was time for me to get up. I sometimes surprised her by getting up before receiving her wake-up call. The radio
would be switched on, waiting for RTE 1 to come on air at 7.30 a.m.
Before this they played classical music, and I got used to listening to the
new-age genre of French composer Jean Michel Jarre with music
taken from his albums *Oxygene* and *Equinoxe*.

My parents and I would all sit down to breakfast together, and God
how pampered I was. I would have either corn flakes or Weetabix with
hot milk, followed by a boiled egg, tea, toast and marmalade as we sat
and listened to the eight o'clock news, followed by *What It Says in the
Papers*. How my breakfast differed to Sands, who wrote about his in one
of his journals, which perhaps illustrated his apathy and subsequent
hunger strike:

> The prospects of cold, tasteless porridge along with two slices of
> bread and half a mug of lukewarm tea was depressing.

'Father, are you going to pour the tea?' I would ask with good reason.
It was always amusing to watch his craftiness, as he had developed a
truly unique way of pouring tea. He used to hold the teapot a distance
away from the mug, pour a little but then stop as he tilted the teapot
upright before starting again and gradually working his way down

until the spout of the teapot reached the rim of the mug before it was full. But he always managed to pour my tea exactly to the strength that I liked it served and never spilt or splashed any of it in the process.

I watched Bobby Sands' funeral on television and was mesmerised that over a hundred thousand mourners attended. I couldn't believe that someone could be so famous for being a terrorist. I also thought it was incredible that, only a few weeks earlier when he had been on hunger strike for nearly five weeks, his skeletal self could get elected as an MP to the British Parliament from a prison cell, making him the youngest person to ever gain this status. Unfortunately, his death prompted the IRA to launch an even more ferocious campaign of violence and destruction in response.

The moment finally came when it was time for me to leave home. September arrived and it was time for me to leave Derrykinlough to start my catering college course in Galway. My childhood was over and the big wide world was waiting to become my oyster! My life adventure was about to begin. I was leaving behind me the green fields of Sligo, school, friends and life on the farm. And although I would often return to Derrykinlough to visit, life there would never seem the same again in view of the changes that were going to occur in me as a result of my new-found independence.

I was all packed and ready to go, and my mother drove me into Charlestown that sunny September morning. I then waited in anticipation for the bus to arrive. On the hour-and-a-half bus journey to Galway, I was seated next to a lecturer from the Regional Technical College that I was to attend. In between listening to stories about his holiday in the Black Forest of Germany, I occasionally glanced out of the window at the countryside. The journey ahead was full of mystery. New friendships and experiences were awaiting me, and upon reflection, the conversation I had with my fellow passenger was the beginning of my discovery of the different viewpoints that would extend my horizons.

And what then? What happened when I reached Galway? How did my life shape out thereafter? Did it unlock the dreams, aspirations and potential that I had in mind? Would I eventually find the ideal job after college? Who would I fall in love with and where would life take me? And what about riches? Happiness even? These unanswered questions remind me of the famous Sligo poet William Butler Yeats, who outlined some of these points in his poem *What Then?*

His chosen comrades thought at school
He must grow a famous man;
He thought the same and lived the rule,
All his twenties crammed with toil;
'What then?' sang Plato's ghost, 'What then?'

Everything he wrote was read,
After certain years he won
Sufficient money for his need,
Friends that have been friends indeed;
'What then?' sang Plato's ghost, 'What then?'

All his happier dreams came true –
A small house, wife, daughter, son.
Grounds where plums and cabbage grew,
Poets and wits about him drew
'What then?' sang Plato's ghost, 'What then?'

'The work is done', grown old he thought
According to my boyish plan;
Lets the fools rage, I swerved in naught,
Something to perfection brought;
But louder sang that ghost, 'What then?'

Most people realise at some point or another that life doesn't turn out quite the way they expected when they were young. The best-laid plans can sometimes fail, but yet life holds rare and wonderful surprises. What one yearns for is sometimes not quite what one needs. Moreover, God is very good at providing alternatives. He has a wealth of substitutes at His disposal, and from the ones I have experienced, I know them to be truly excellent.

It is easy for me to say that I believe being Irish is more than a nationality, more than a cultural identity, it is like being part of a dynasty with a reassurance that I shall never be separated from this because it is firmly ingrained in my psyche. But if I were to identify the most important lesson that I took away from my Irish childhood and upbringing, I would choose a sense of decency in life, an appreciation of knowing when to do the right thing. And with this I left my childhood in Derrykinlough behind and travelled to Galway to face the many sunrises and sunsets of life that lay before me.

Acknowledgements

I would like to thank a little army of people who helped in one way or another to make the publication of *Buried Deep in My Heart* possible.

Much appreciation to Simon Kelly, my publisher, and his team at The London Press for their incredible professionalism. This is the second time we have worked together and once again I have found Simon's knowledge of the book trade both helpful and reassuring.

Special thanks to Allen Horsman, my editor and proof-reader, for his professionalism and trusted attention to detail.

Many thanks also to Joe Byrne at Midwest Radio in Ireland for the time he took in his busy schedule to write an introduction to the book.

I would also like to give special mention to Phyl Flannery and the Leyney writers in Tubbercurry for previewing the manuscript and providing valuable feedback.

I wish to give recognition to my brother Kevin for taking most of the photographs featured in the book. Taking photographs with a Kodak camera that had a 126mm film complete with flash cubes in tow sometimes created much fun, but the process was mesmerisingly prolonged in comparison to today's digital age, especially when the camera shutter jammed or the flash cube failed to go off. There is nothing worse than to be in pose mode and for the camera to fail to do its job!

Last, but not least, many thanks go to my artist friend Hayley McAuley, who was terrific in helping me arrange the photographs featured in the book. From hundreds of old photographs and negatives I short-listed 80 images before eventually whittling this down to 41 in the final edit. Hayley also kindly designed the website for the book, which can be viewed at: www.burieddeepinmyheart.co.uk

Once again my sincere thanks to all involved behind the scenes.

About the Author

Declan Henry was born in County Sligo, Ireland. Educated at Goldsmiths' College and King's College, London, he has published a collection of fictional stories about disaffected teenagers, *Glimpses* (The London Press, 2007). His other publications have appeared in magazines and newspapers in both Ireland and the UK: *Community Care, Sligo Weekender, National Children's Bureau magazine, The Kent Journal of Mental Health, Medway News, The Write Angel.* Declan also writes a monthly column for *The Irish Community News.* His website www.declanhenry.co.uk contains a collection of twenty-three new and previously published social work and non-fictional articles – as well as a fiction section with short stories and a novelette. Declan holds a Master of Science Degree in Mental Health Social Work and Bachelor of Arts (Hons) Degree in Education and Community Studies. His first career was in the hotel and catering industry, which saw him receive a double distinction in the City & Guilds exams at catering college, the only student out of a group of sixty-four to achieve this success. Declan then went on to work in five-star hotels and private clubs in Ireland, France, Switzerland, Australia and England – as well as working as an airline steward for two years. He is a registered social worker and has worked in the profession since 1993. He currently works with young offenders, many of whom have multiple and complex needs. Declan lives in Kent, England.